INDOOR ACTION GAMES FOR ELEMENTARY CHILDREN

Active Games and Academic Activities for Fun and Fitness

David R. Foster
Chico Unified School District

James L. Overholt, Ed. D.
California State University, Chico

Illustrations by Ron Schultz

PARKER PUBLISHING COMPANY
West Nyack, New York 10995

Lp

ISBN 0-13-459124-0

PARKER PUBLISHING COMPANY
BUSINESS & PROFESSIONAL DIVISION
A division of Simon & Schuster
West Nyack, New York 10995

Foster, David R.
    Indoor action games for elementary children.

    1. Physical education for children.   2. Indoor
games. I. Overholt, James L.   II. Schultz, Ron.
III. Title.
GV443.F65 1989 613.7′042   88-33028
ISBN 0-13-459124-0

Library of Congress Cataloging-in-Publication Data

ABOUT THIS RESOURCE

We are convinced that there can be more to rainy-day recess and physical education sessions than "Eraser Tag" and "Free Time." Our purpose is to provide elementary school teachers and physical education instructors with a variety of effective indoor recess/physical education activities. This book provides a large number of both active and academic alternatives for teachers who are expected to control and motivate restless children during an indoor school day. It can also serve as a valuable resource for parents, recreation directors, camp counselors, and others who spend time with young people.

That physical education is an essential part of the overall education of elementary school students, is well documented and widely accepted among educators. Daily participation in physical activities by students is important for several reasons: the development of health and fitness; to provide an outlet for the release of tension accumulated during a strenuous academic school day; the improvement of skills necessary for mental and physical development; to prompt the development of interests which contribute to a happier and healthier adult life; and to provide the recreation necessary for elementary school students to remain academically productive throughout the school day.

Research shows that there is a positive correlation between physical activity and academic success. Students who are given the chance to engage in physical activity periodically throughout the school day work more efficiently, and accomplish more, than students who are denied the opportunity of stimulating exercises.

The need for physical activity does not diminish or disappear during periods of inclement weather. In fact, as teachers, physical educators, and parents are well aware, children who are forced to remain indoors on school days desperately need frequent chances for recreation if they are to remain orderly and academically productive. Indoor school days generally make students fidgety, restless, and more disruptive than usual. Concentration and cooperation tend to deteriorate as the indoor school day wears on. This situation can be unproductive for students and extremely exasperating for teachers. Teachers work very hard to maintain their students' academic excellence throughout the school year. The goals of the activities presented herein are to help teachers continue to provide a quality learning environment, and to enhance student health and fitness, on those often troublesome, inclement weather school days.

This book is a collection of many newly created activities and some of the best old games for indoor recess/physical education periods in elementary school classrooms. It is not meant to replace an existing physical education curriculum; rather, it is intended as a helpful and enjoyable supplement for teachers and physical educators to use during periods of inclement weather. The emphasis is on active games which can be played in a limited amount of space (although many may also be played in a multipurpose room or gymnasium), with a minimal amount of equipment and preparation. Some of the activities have been written using the pronoun she, and others with he, but all of the games may be played by either boys or girls. Also included are a collection of less active games; a number of which involve academic content from various subjects.

It is intended that students who participate in the activities will thoroughly enjoy themselves, and as a result remain attentive and academically productive throughout inclement weather school days. The book will also help to make indoor school days more enjoyable and satisfying for teachers, physical educators, and others who work with young people.

David R. Foster
James L. Overholt

ABOUT THE AUTHORS

David R. Foster, M.Ed. (California State University, Chico) currently teaches sixth grade at Parkview Elementary School in Chico, California. Previously, he served as a fifth and sixth grade teacher at Fairview Elementary School in Orland, California, and at Terrace Middle School, Lakeport, California, and worked as a student aide in grades 4 through 6. Mr. Foster has also coached boys' and girls' volleyball, basketball, and baseball and did his Master's thesis on the subject of "Indoor Physical Education/Recess Activities for Elementary School Classrooms."

James L. Overholt, Ed.D. (University of Wyoming, Laramie) has over 20 years of experience as an elementary teacher and educator. He began his career teaching in the public schools of LeSueur and Albert Lea, Minnesota, then served as a mathematics teacher/coordinator and instructor in Elementary Education at the University School, University of Wyoming. Presently, Dr. Overholt is Professor of Teacher Education at California State University, Chico, where he specializes in the areas of student teaching, in-service education, and mathematics education.

SUGGESTIONS FOR USING
INDOOR ACTION GAMES

The activities in this book have been categorized by grade level and purpose(s) for your convenience. However, you, as the teacher and/or physical education instructor, are ultimately the most qualified person to determine appropriate activities for your particular group of students. Thus, since many of the activities can be successfully implemented for any age or grade level (e.g., Snowshoe Race), please do make use of each activity in as many ways as possible.

We also urge users of this book to give careful consideration to the suggested variations included for each activity. You will find that many of the variations foster enthusiasm and continued interest by the students.

As fellow teachers, we realize the importance of offering activities that require minimal preparation and equipment. These factors were given careful consideration throughout the book. Several of the activities require some basic and easily obtainable materials (e.g., paper plates, foam rubber ball, balloons) and, conveniently, many require identical equipment. Therefore, by locating or making the simple pieces of equipment necessary for some of the activities (see the Appendix), you will be able to effectively utilize the activities in this book, and will wisely have spent a minimal amount of time in preparation.

We would also like to offer a safety caution. The games herein are quite safe; however, it is always wise to establish and enforce regulations for safe play. As such, we recommend that the involved teacher or leader adhere to guidelines such as:

- Promote cooperation, self-testing, and self-improvement, rather than competition.
- State and/or review safety rules prior to beginning any activity (e.g., no pushing or touching unless specifically called for in the game).
- Note a signal that will "freeze" everyone in position if a dangerous situation should occur (e.g., blowing a whistle or turning out the lights).
- Closely enforce all guidelines during the initial time period.

Many of the activities in this book will cause students to become excited. In such instances, the "noise level" will likely go up. Thus, we suggest that you plan to do your *Indoor Action Games* during the same time periods as the teacher(s) next door; such pre-planning for the consideration of others will also help to establish harmony among the teaching staff.

Finally, it is understood that some classrooms are not as spacious as others. With this in mind, we have designed a number of the activities so that they may be played with the desks in place or you may prefer to take a few moments to arrange the room in a way that allows the maximum amount of space. In addition, most of the activities can also be played in a multi-purpose room or gymnasium. So organize in the manner which will work best for your class—and let the fun begin!!!

TABLE OF CONTENTS

SECTION	*** GRADE LEVEL ***			*** PURPOSE ***								
	K–2	2–4	4–6	Just for Fun	Lead up Activities	Cooperation Games	Team Competition	Physical Fitness	Academic Activities	Coordination/Agility	Flexibility	
I. "Getting to Know You" Games												1
Instant Replay	X	X	X	X								3
Tennis Ball Hello	X	X	X	X					X			4
You're in the Spotlight	X	X	X	X								5
Signature Scramble	X	X	X	X				X				6
Odd Bean Social	X	X						X	X			7
Grab a Flag	X	X	X	X	X			X		X	X	8
Go Fly an Airplane	X	X	X	X						X		9
Balloon Introductions	X	X	X	X						X		10
Musical Madness	X	X	X	X		X				X		11
Ping Pong Information	X	X	X	X						X		12
Name Buzz	X	X	X	X					X			13
If I Were	X	X	X	X					X	X		14
Did You Catch My Name?	X	X	X	X						X		15
Birthday Bash		X	X	X					X			16
II. Cooperative Challenges												17
Magic Bridges	X					X	X					19
Cat and Rat	X					X	X					20
Animal Parade	X			X				X				21
Herd Hunt	X					X						22
I Saw	X	X		X				X				23
The Balancing Act	X	X		X		X				X		24
Animal Chase	X	X				X				X		25
Hide It and Seek It	X	X		X		X						26
Indoor Golf	X	X	X		X	X				X	X	27
Balloon Bop	X	X	X			X	X			X		28
Paper Plate Disk Toss	X	X	X			X				X		29
Sponge or Treasure	X	X	X	X						X		30
Detective	X	X	X	X			X					31
Ringer	X	X	X	X	X					X		32
We're Really Rollin' Now	X	X	X			X				X		33
What a Drag	X	X	X	X		X		X				34

x

I
"GETTING TO KNOW YOU" GAMES

INSTANT REPLAY

Grades: K–6

Purposes: To help students become familiar with their classmates' names and personalities
To have fun

Equipment: None

Description: After clearing desks from the center of the room, have players form a large circle. One person starts by moving a few steps into the center and announcing his name while performing whatever movements and gestures he chooses. For instance, one might skip into the center and perform a grand sweeping wave of the hand, proclaiming to all, "Andy," and skip back to his place in the circle. That is the signal for everyone else to do exactly as he did, in unison, mimicking him in both deed and word as closely as possible. Repeat the procedure until all players have had a chance to introduce themselves.

Variations: Have a player move into the center and announce a word that describes himself (funny, smart, fast, etc.).

TENNIS BALL HELLO

Grades: K–6

Purposes: To improve hand-eye coordination
To help students learn each other's names and reveal each person's favorite activities
To have fun

Equipment: One tennis ball or any non-threatening ball

Description: This game can be played while sitting on desktops or while sitting or standing in a circle. The teacher starts the game by tossing the ball to a student, whereupon he introduces himself and announces his favorite game or activity. When a player is finished, he tosses the ball to someone else, who then repeats the procedure. The game is over when each player has introduced himself.

Variations: (1) Play several rounds by having players call out favorite food, musical group, place to go, and so on. (2) Have participants act out a motion for each player's favorite sport or game (pretend to swing a bat for baseball).

YOU'RE IN THE SPOTLIGHT

Grades: K–6

Purposes: To help students find out about each other
To have lots of fun

Equipment: A flashlight (any similar object can be substituted)

Description: Have the group form a circle, sitting down, with one player in the middle holding a flashlight. Make the room as dark as possible by closing curtains and turning out the lights. The person in the middle puts the flashlight on the floor and gives it a spin. The person who is "In the Spotlight" when the flashlight comes to a stop must introduce himself and tell the others one thing about himself. That person then goes to the middle and becomes the next spinner. Toward the end of the game, players may simply point the light at someone that hasn't been introduced.

Variations: (1) Play several rounds and change the information to be announced (favorite band, best quality, weirdest dream, etc.). (2) Allow the spinner to ask the person "In the Spotlight" a particular question instead of establishing the required response ahead of time.

SIGNATURE SCRAMBLE*

Grades: K–6

Purposes: To allow students to mingle and interact
To provide mild exercise

Equipment: A sheet of paper and pencil for each player

Description: Give each player a sheet of paper and instruct him/her to fold it into a certain number of squares, depending on grade level. The object is for each player to gather as many *legible* signatures as possible in a given amount of time. Each signature must be clearly written in one of the squares to be legitimate. The first person to fill his or her sheet is the winner.

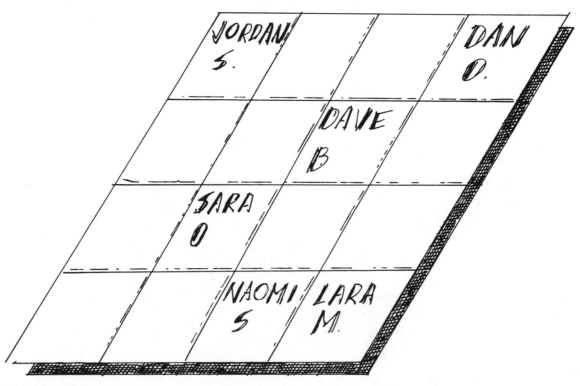

Variations: (1) Make the task easier for younger students by having them print first name only or just one letter or number, etc. (2) Increase the difficulty for older students by requiring a signature and a complete sentence, math problem, etc. (3) Add a task to the original activity. For example, after a player gets the required signatures, he must run the 440 low hurdles (walk quickly around the room 4 times while jumping over 4 chairs placed an equal distance apart).

---

*Art Kamiya, *The Elementary Teacher Handbook of Indoor and Outdoor Games* (West Nyack, N.Y.: Parker Publishing Co., Inc., 1985)

ODD BEAN SOCIAL*

Grades: K–6

Purposes: To practice counting and addition
To reinforce the concept of odd and even numbers
To provide mild exercise
To allow students to mingle

Equipment: Ten to twenty beans or similar objects for each player

Description: Give each person an equal number of beans. Players walk around the room in a random pattern, and when two players wish, they stop and begin an interaction. One player holds out a closed hand containing a certain number of beans and asks, "Odd or even?" If the other player answers correctly, he gets the beans. If the person guesses erroneously, he must give the opponent that number of beans. The object is to have the greatest number of beans at the end of the time period.

Variations: (1) For younger students, have them guess the number of beans in the hand instead of odd/even. (2) Have both players hold out a handful of beans, one player call odd/even, add the total number of beans to determine the outcome, and the loser pays the highest number of beans held by one player.

*Art Kamiya, *The Elementary Teacher Handbook of Indoor and Outdoor Games* (West Nyack, N.Y.: Parker Publishing Co., Inc., 1985)

GRAB A FLAG

Grades: K–6

Purposes: To help students become familiar with each other's names and favorite activities
To enhance quickness and agility
To have a great time

Equipment: Each student will need a pencil and a strip of paper or cloth, about three inches wide by twelve inches long

Description: Have each student write her (or his) name and at least three favorite activities on her flag. Then tuck one end of the flag under the student's waistband or belt or paper clip it to her clothing. Next, have all of the students scatter themselves around the room or play area. At the "go" signal, each player attempts to grab and keep another student's flag. This continues until the leader commands "captured flags freeze." Those with the captured flags hold them high and freeze in position. Then, anyone without a flag may take any previously uncaptured flag. As soon as they all have flags, the students are to take turns introducing the person whose flag they captured, and also ask that person questions about their favorite activities.

Variations: (1) Make the task easier for younger students by having them print only their first names or, if necessary, having an adult do the writing for them. (2) At the end of the activity, for older students, all the flags can be gathered together. Then, the leader should call out several of the named favorite activities, and the players must try to identify the person(s) who like those activities.

GO FLY AN AIRPLANE

Grades: K–6

Purposes: To help students to get to know each other
To enhance small and large motor skills
To have fun

Equipment: A sheet of paper and a pencil or crayons for each player

Description: Each student is to construct a paper airplane. Once it is folded, he needs to write his (or her) name and several facts about himself on the plane. He may also use crayons to decorate it. Next, have the students stand along the walls. At the command "take-off" all of the students must launch their airplanes toward the center of the room. Any airplanes landing on desks are to remain there, but any on the floor need to be placed on the closest desks. Airplanes whose placements are not certain may be launched a second time. The students are then to return to their own desks, find out whose airplane they have, and introduce that person.

Variations: (1) Young students may need help to complete their airplanes. (2) To complete the activity more quickly, the information may be written on sheets of paper, formed into crumpled paper balls, and thrown in the same manner.

BALLOON INTRODUCTIONS

Grades: K–6

Purposes: To acquaint students with each other
To provide physical activity
To have an enjoyable time

Equipment: A balloon for each student, pens to mark on them, and a container large enough to hold all of the inflated balloons

Description: Give each student a balloon to blow up or inflate them in advance. Have the students use the marking pens to write their names on the balloons and decorate them in any way they wish. The leader then gathers all of the balloons into a container, such as a large plastic bag or box, and takes them to the highest point in the room. All of the balloons are released at once and, as they fall, the students repeatedly bat them into the air. After a brief time, the leader commands "capture a balloon." Then each student catches a balloon and "freezes" in position. As soon as everyone has a balloon, the leader calls on a student to introduce the person whose balloon she has captured. The named student must stand and tell something about herself. When finished, she introduces the student whose balloons he has captured. This procedure continues until everyone has been introduced.

Variations: (1) Young students may need help to inflate their balloons and/or to write their names on them. (2) In order to disperse the balloons widely, they may be released in front of a functioning air vent or fan.

MUSICAL MADNESS

Grades: K–6

Purposes: To help students get to know one another
To promote cooperation
To have lots of fun

Equipment: A few hoops, old bicycle tires, or large pieces of butcher paper
A radio, tape player, or record player

Description: Place several hoops or tires randomly about the play area. Play some lively music while players walk briskly around the room. When the music stops, all players quickly get to the nearest hoop and attempt to get some body part inside the hoop. Remove one of the hoops after each round so that the game becomes more and more challenging, and more fun!

Variations: (1) Change the method of locomotion to be used while the music plays (hop, skip, crab walk, etc.) (2) As hoops are removed, have the players from the hoops tell something about themselves (name, favorite place to visit, best quality, etc.).

PING PONG INFORMATION

Grades: K–6

Purposes: To informally acquaint students with their classmates' names and/or favorite activities
To provide practice bouncing a ping pong ball

Equipment: A ping pong ball for each group

Description: Organize the students in groups of 5 to 8 (or the entire class can play as one large group). Then have each group sit on the floor in a circle with each person's legs spread apart in a V-shape and their feet touching both neighbors. When the group is in position, drop a ping pong ball in the center and let it bounce until it stops between some person's legs. That person must pick up the ball, state her (or his) name, toss the ball into the air again, and tell something about herself before it stops bouncing. Play continues in this manner until each person has had one or more turns.

Variations: When receiving the ping pong ball, have the player state what the previous person's name and trait were before giving his (her) own name and favorite activity.

NAME BUZZ

Grades: K–6

Purposes: To acquaint the students with each other's names and/or favorite activities
To practice counting and recognizing multiples

Equipment: None

Description: Have the entire class stand in a large circle or along the walls of the classroom. The leader specifies a multiple (such as four) where a student, instead of counting, is to call out his or her name and favorite activity, food, etc. A designated student begins by counting aloud "one" and does one quick exercise (such as one hop), the next person says "two" and does two activities (as touching toes two times), and the third person counts "three" and completes three consecutive movements. Then for example, if Brian is the fourth person, he should say something like, "My name is Brian, and I like to play football." Play then continues to the fifth person who does five activities (as nodding his head five times), and the sixth and seventh respectively. When the count comes to the eighth person, Susan might say, "I'm Susan, and I have a collection of Raggedy Ann and Andy dolls." This procedure can continue to a specific number (as 89 or 314) or for a designated length of time.

Variations: (1) Beginning students might count only to the designated multiple. That is, if the multiple is 5, the counting would be done as 1, 2, 3, 4, and "My name is Ben and I like to go fishing with my grandpa." Then the next person would begin counting with 1 again, etc. (2) Advanced students might count by multiples only. For example, count by 3's and have every person who is a multiple of 9 make a statement; that is 3, 6, and "I'm Sara and I like to play guitar," 12, 15, "my handle is Daniel and I own a spaniel," 21, etc.

IF I WERE

Grades: K–6

Purposes: To get to know each other
To learn to give and guess non-verbal clues
To have a great time

Equipment: None

Description: This pantomime activity can be played in groups or as a whole class. The IF I WERE pantomimes can focus on a wide variety of topics such as animals, movie actors, spelling words, favorite sports, etc. For example, if animals were the focus, the first player would say, "If I were a _____, I would act like this." Then, if the player decided to be a horse, she (or he) will pantomine the actions of a horse, and the other players will try to guess what animal she is portraying.

Variations: Have several players cooperate in a group pantomime. For example, if animals were again the focus, the group leader would state, "If we were _____, we would act like this." Then, if wild geese were to be portrayed, the group might portray flight in a V-formation, and the other players would attempt identification.

DID YOU CATCH MY NAME?

Grades: K–6

Purposes: To help students get to know one another and learn each other's names
To improve hand/eye coordination
To improve memory skills

Equipment: A ball for each group

Description: Have players form groups of five to ten. Groups form circles in different parts of the room. To begin, each player announces his/her name to the group. Then the group decides on a way to pass the ball (bounce pass, roll, behind the back toss, etc.). Players must say their own name and the name of the player to whom they are tossing the ball. The round is over when each player has had a couple of turns. Then players form new groups consisting of different teammates. The process is repeated until everyone has had a chance to participate with everyone in the entire group.

Variations: (1) To start things off, the ball might be tossed around a circle consisting of all the members of the group, and the whole group calls out the name of the person who catches the ball. (2) Add another detail to the game after everyone learns names (favorite pet, best subject in school, birthday, etc.).

BIRTHDAY BASH

Grades: 2–6

Purposes: To help students get to know one another
To promote cooperation

Equipment: None

Description: Begin the game by having everyone in the room scramble to get together with others who share the same month of birth. After the scramble is over, give teams two to three minutes to come up with some sort of cheer for their month. Each group is then given a chance to present their cheer to the rest of the class.

Variations: (1) Try using different groupings (favorite sport out of football, baseball, basketball, volleyball; favorite seasons or holidays; favorite subject at school, etc.). (2) Try a round in which players can use only non-verbal forms of communication to place themselves in groups (pretending to throw or catch a ball for baseball, making a shot for basketball, etc.).

II

COOPERATIVE CHALLENGES

MAGIC BRIDGES

Grades: K–2

Purposes: To promote cooperation
To provide exercise for overall fitness

Equipment: None

Description: Six or more children are chosen to make bridges. A bridge is made by two children standing facing each other, clasping hands and raising arms. Start the game with three or four bridges placed in the aisles, in front, or in back of the room. The other children walk, skip or run to music, up and down the aisles, around the room, going under the bridges. Every so often, the music stops, and the children who are the bridges lower their arms and try to catch a player as he goes under their bridge. All the players caught form new bridges and the game continues. The last player caught is the winner. If a player, when caught, has no partner to make a bridge with him, he stays out of the game until the music stops again.

Variations: Have children sing a song instead of playing a record. For this version, the leader blows a whistle to activate the bridges.

CAT AND RAT

Grades: K–2

Purposes: To promote group cooperation
To provide exercise for overall fitness

Equipment: None

Description: Push the desks aside. Have players form a circle, hands clasped. One player is chosen for the Cat and one for the Rat. Cat stands outside the circle, Rat stands inside. Cat says, "I am the cat." Rat says, "I am the rat." Cat says, "I will catch you." Rat says, "You cannot." Cat tries to catch Rat. Both must run in and out of the circle and around the circle, while circle players help Rat by raising their arms to let him run under. They try to stop Cat from breaking through the circle. When Rat is caught, other children are chosen to take the places of Cat and Rat.

Variations: (1) Have children form smaller groups to allow several games to be played at the same time. (2) Play the game with two sets of Cats and Rats.

ANIMAL PARADE

Grades: K–2

Purposes: To reinforce knowledge of animal names and their sounds
To have a great time

Equipment: None

Description: Have the children form a circle. Choose one person to be the leader. The leader calls the name of a child and names an animal. The child does an imitation of the movements of the animal named. After everyone has had a chance to imitate an animal, all of the players form a line for an "Animal Parade" led by the leader. The group moves around the room, each imitating the animal he represents.

Variations: Play a round with sound imitations only, then play a combination round with movements and sounds.

HERD HUNT

Grades: K–2

Purposes: To promote group cooperation
To divide players into smaller groups in preparation for other activities

Equipment: None

Description: This is a technique for dividing a group into teams or smaller groups, but is a game in itself as well. Have players stand in a circle with their eyes closed. They must keep their eyes closed throughout the activity. The leader goes from person to person whispering the name of an animal in their ears; they must remember their animal. After the leader has given each child the name of an animal, all players make the noises that their animal makes and while keeping their eyes closed, find the other members of their species. When all species have grouped, the game is finished. The leader may want to give different animals and have the group play another round.

Variations: Use sounds other than animal sounds (different types of machinery, etc.).

I SAW

Grades: K–4

Purposes: To develop non-verbal communication skills
To have a great time

Equipment: None

Description: Have one child stand in front of the room, or have the children form a circle with one child in the center. The child who is chosen says, "On my way to school this morning I saw..." and then imitates what she saw. The others guess what she saw by her imitation. The one guessing correctly goes to the front or center, and the game continues in the same manner. If no one guesses, the one in the center or in front tells what she was imitating and then selects someone else to take her place.

Variations: Use different topics: "At the zoo I saw..."; "On vacation I saw..."; "While I was playing at the park I saw..."; etc.

THE BALANCING ACT

Grades: K–4

Purposes: To provide practice in movement and balance
To promote cooperation

Equipment: A beanbag, eraser, or similar object for each player.
A tape player and tape or a record player and record.

Description: Have each player balance an object on his/her head. Play music while players walk around the room balancing the object on their heads. If the object falls off, the person is frozen until a friend comes by and replaces the object on the frozen player's head. Everyone stops and resets when the music stops. Repeat the process several times.

Variations: (1) Play the game in groups of three to five, in which case, if any of the players in a group drops the object from his head, the whole group is frozen until another group comes by to help. (2) Change the method of locomotion (walk backwards, shuffle, skip, etc.).

ANIMAL CHASE

Grades: K–4

Purposes: To develop quickness, coordination and concentration
To promote cooperation
To reinforce the knowledge of animal names and sounds

Equipment: Several miscellaneous classroom objects

Description: Have the children form a circle, fairly close together, sitting or standing, facing each other. Using erasers, beanbags, small balls, etc., the leader presents an object to the children to be given an animal's name. The "animal" is then passed around the circle and back to the leader, who starts it around again, this time sending another "animal" out to chase him. The game is made progressively harder by increasing the number of objects sent around the circle, by varying them as to shape and size, and by changing direction of the pass.

Variations: (1) Have the children play a round with their eyes closed. (2) Have players imitate the appropriate animal sounds as objects are being passed. (3) Have the children perform a task each time one animal catches up with another, or when an animal is dropped (five push-ups, jog around the classroom, 10 jumping-jacks, etc.).

HIDE IT AND SEEK IT

Grades: K–4

Purposes: To promote group cooperation
To have a great time

Equipment: Any miscellaneous classroom object

Description: Show all of the players the object to be hidden, then choose a hunter to leave the room. After the hunter leaves the room, the object is hidden; the hunter is then called back into the room to hunt for it. As a hint to the hunter as to his nearness to the object, the group claps loudly when he is near and softly when he is far away. When the hunter finds the object, he chooses another hunter, and the game continues.

Variations: (1) Use a different technique for giving hints to the hunter (soft and loud humming, raising and lowering of hands, soft and loud finger snapping, etc.). (2) Have two hunters and make it a race to find the object (assign half the group to give hints to one hunter, the other children direct their hints toward the other hunter). (3) Using a large object (trash can, globe, etc.), have the hunter try to find the object with his eyes closed.

INDOOR GOLF

Grades: K–6

Purposes: To improve hand/eye coordination
To improve throwing accuracy

Equipment: One beanbag or wad of scrap paper per player
Nine large tin cans or containers numbered 1 through 9.

Description: Have players form groups of two while the teacher or students place cans about the room. Each pair of players starts at the "hole" (tin can) and throws their beanbags into the next "hole" in sequence. Players keep track of the total number of shots taken to complete each hole. At the end of nine holes, players add the total shots taken and the winner is the player with the lowest total. If time allows, have players repeat the procedure.

Variations: (1) Allow players only one shot per "hole," giving one point for each shot made. (2) Have the players complete a game using trick shots (between the legs, behind the back, etc.). (3) Play more than one game to see if players can improve their scores.

BALLOON BOP*

Grades: K–6

Purposes: To improve hand/eye and foot/eye coordination
To reinforce counting skills
To promote team work and cooperation

Equipment: Several balloons

Description: Arrange the desks so that several groups can form circles. Players may stand or sit to play this game. Each team is given one inflated balloon which they are to keep in the air for as long as possible. Team members bat or tap the balloon with their hands; no throwing or catching is allowed. Each time the balloon hits the ground, score one point against the team that failed to keep it in the air. The team with the lowest score at the end of the given time period wins the game.

Variations: (1)Divide the group into smaller teams and have several teams competing at the same time. (2) Have players use their feet instead of their hands to keep the balloon in the air. (3) Have team members count aloud the number of times the balloon is hit without touching the ground. (4) For older students, have players count by 3's, 5's, or 10's.

---

*Cotler, Harold L., *Galaxy of Games, Stunts, and Activities for Elementary Physical Education*, West Nyack, NY: Parker Publishing Company, Inc., 1980.

PAPER PLATE DISK TOSS

Grades: K–6

Purposes: To improve hand/eye coordination
To promote group cooperation

Equipment: One paper plate for each child
One or more boxes

Description: Have each child write his (her) name on a paper plate, and then have all of the students assemble in an open area of the classroom. Place a large box in the open area and mark a line with chalk, tape, or chairs an adequate distance from the box on all four sides. One player begins the game by trying to toss his disk into the box, and one by one, each child takes a turn. After each has had a turn, players retrieve their disk one section at a time. Players keep track of the total number of times their disk lands in the box. The winner is the one with the most successful throws at the end of a designated time period.

Variations: (1)Play a "Speed Toss" round in which players throw as many times as they can in a minute. In this version, players must retrieve their disks quickly so as not to interfere with other players' tosses. (2) Use two or three boxes and have smaller groups. (3) Have players throw with their non-dominant hand. (4) Vary the distance from which players toss the disks.

SPONGE OR TREASURE

Grades: K–6

Purposes: To have a great time
To improve quickness and throwing skills

Equipment: A supply of soft sponges or foam rubber balls

Description: The classroom is marked off into three zones: a treasure zone, a guard zone, and seekers zone. A "treasure" (book, ball, or any object) is placed on a desk in the treasure zone at one end of the room. Two, three or four students are designated as "treasure guards," and each is provided with a supply of sponges or foam rubber balls. These guards are to patrol the guard zone in the center section of the room. Two to four additional students may be designated "judges." The rest of the students are "treasure seekers," and they must remain in the seekers zone until the treasure search command is given. The object is for the treasure seekers to get past the guards and touch the treasure without being hit by a sponge. The first seekers to touch the treasure become the guards for the next round.

Variations: (1) Close the drapes or blinds, turn off the lights, and play the game in semi-darkness. (2) Play a game where more guards are used and the treasure seekers must be hit twice in order to be out of the competition.

DETECTIVE

Grades: K–6

Purposes: To improve memory and recall skills
To help develop an eye for detail

Equipment: None

Description: Divide the group into two equal teams. Teams line up two to three feet apart, facing each other. One team is chosen to be the detective team and has sixty seconds to closely observe everything about their respective partners from the opposing team. After the time limit expires, the members of the detective team turn around and shut their eyes while the other players change one thing about their appearance (untie one shoe, move a piece of jewelry, untuck shirt, etc.). When everyone is ready, the detectives turn around, and one at a time try to identify what has been changed on their partner. The game can be played just for fun, or a score may be kept counting each correct response as a point. The teams reverse roles, and the game continues.

Variations: (1) Play a round where players who have their change identified must perform a task (hop around the room twice, run in place for thirty seconds, etc.). (2) Play a round with only one detective assigned to two members of the opposing team to increase the challenge.

RINGER!

Grades: K–6

Purposes: To promote cooperation
To improve hand/eye coordination
To serve as a lead-up game for horseshoes

Equipment: Several rubber, foam rubber or wooden horseshoes, or rings made of rope or old garden hose

Description: Have players form groups of four (or more if equipment is limited). Teams line up at opposite ends of the room, with a desk in front of each team. One of the legs of the desk is designated as the scoring peg, or both legs facing the opposing team can be "in play." Players throw the horseshoes and the scoring can be the same as regular horseshoes, or a more lenient scoring system can be implemented to allow more scoring. Play the game for fun, or set a point total to be reached.

Variations: (1) Have the players turn the desks upside down and use rings to loop the legs. (2) On tile floors, players can play a round in which they slide horseshoes toward the peg rather than throw them.

WE'RE REALLY ROLLIN' NOW

Grades: K–6

Purposes: To improve hand/eye coordination
To promote cooperation

Equipment: A penny, poker chip, or any similar round object for each player

Description: Have players form groups of five to eight. Each groups forms a large circle, and a small circle is drawn in the middle of each group (chalk or tape can be used to make the circle). Each player is given a round object, which they roll toward the circle one at a time, in an attempt to roll their object so that it stops inside the circle. When more than one player successfully rolls the object into the circle on a given round, the one closest to the center wins the point. Play for fun or establish a point total necessary to win the game.

Variations: (1) Play a round in which players toss their objects toward the circle rather than roll them (regular toss; under the leg; turn around, bend over, and toss through the legs; over the shoulder, etc.). (2) Play a round in which players close their eyes and roll or toss the object toward the circle. (3) Have different stations (roll station, toss station, roll-with-the-foot station) and have players rotate around the room.

WHAT A DRAG

Grades: K–6

Purposes: To promote cooperation
To develop strength and endurance

Equipment: Several old sheets or blankets

Description: Arrange the desks to allow wide aisles for relay teams. Have players form teams of six to ten. Players form pairs within their teams. The object is for one player to drag his/her partner (who is sitting or lying on a sheet or blanket) to the end of the room and back. The two switch jobs, and the process is repeated. Each pair completes the same task, until each player has had a chance to drag and be dragged.

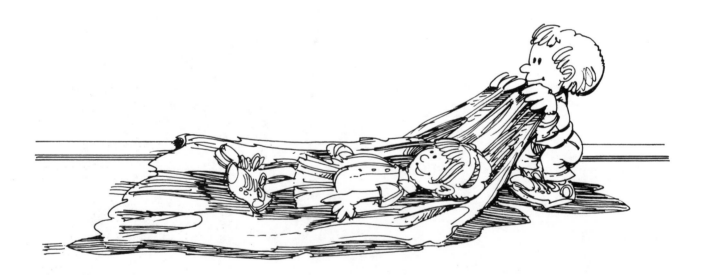

Variations: (1) Increase the number of people on the blanket and have more draggers pulling them (2) Have the entire team get on the blanket and attempt to move down and back by scooting, rolling, shuffling, etc.

JUST A TOUCH

Grades: K–6

Purposes: To promote cooperation
To improve hand/eye coordination

Equipment: Several tennis balls for each group
Some plastic soft drink containers (such as 2-liter Coke bottles)

Description: Divide the players into teams of four to six. Set numbered plastic containers at different points in the play area. Players are to follow the numbered course in order. Start each team at a different location to eliminate waiting. Mark one tennis ball for each group to identify it as Ball #1. The first player for each team rolls Ball #1 toward the designated plastic bottle from a specified distance. Then each following team member rolls another ball and attempts to bump or nudge Ball #1 closer to the bottle; the object is to get Ball #1 to touch the plastic bottle without knocking it over. When the bottle is touched, the team moves on to the next numbered bottle, but if it is knocked over, the team might be required to try a second time. The game can be played just for fun or a scoring system can be devised, such as 3 points for each bottle touched, but only 1 point if it is knocked over.

Variations: (1) For older players, have a round where all shots must be bank shots (must hit a wall or piece of furniture before making contact with Ball #1). (2) Play a round where all shots are made by rolling the ball by foot (be certain that players don't kick the ball; instead they are to roll it along the bottom of their foot, releasing it at the heel).

KEEP IT UP

Grades: 2–6

Purposes: To promote cooperation
To improve coordination

Equipment: One beach ball or balloon

Description: Push desks aside. One circle of people lies on the floor, side by side, knees bent, and hands in the air. A second circle of people stands outside of the group that is lying down. They toss the beach ball, and the group lying down tries to keep the ball in the air, without letting it touch the ground. Each time it touches the ground, the outside team may score one point. After a certain score, or time period, switch positions.

Variation: Use more than one beach ball.

THREE-BALL BLAST

Grades: 2–6

Purposes: To improve overall physical fitness
To improve quickness and agility
To improve throwing and catching skills

Equipment: Three foam rubber balls marked with the numbers 1, 2, and 3 (Wadded up rags or towels may be substituted for foam balls)

Description: Mark the objects to be used with a number 1 on one ball, a number 2 on another ball, and a number 3 on the remaining ball. Move the desks enough to allow aisle space for the base paths of a small baseball diamond. Place pieces of scratch paper down at the appropriate spots to indicate bases. Divide the group into two teams; one team is up to bat, while the other team's players scatter about the room. The first batter picks up the three balls and throws them, one at a time, anywhere in the room (there is no such thing as a foul ball). The player then walks as fast as he can around the basepath being careful to touch each base. The batter keeps going until the fielding team manages to get each ball to the proper base (#1 on 1st base, #2 on second, and #3 on third base). A point is scored for the batting team for each base touched before all balls arrive at the proper bases. All players on the batting team take a turn (rather than the three-out system), then the teams switch places and the game continues.

Variations: (1) Have the players kick the balls rather than throw them. (2) Play a round where the batter must be hit by all three balls to stop his progress, rather than throwing the balls to the bases.

QUIET BALL

Grades: 2–6

Purposes: To improve hand/eye coordination
To promote cooperation

Equipment: One or more foam rubber balls or playground balls

Description: Have all students sit on top of desks. The foam rubber ball is tossed from player to player in a random pattern. If a child catches the ball, she throws it to another person. If a child misses the ball, she must sit back down in her chair and becomes a blocker. If a player that has been eliminated manages to block the toss of another player, she is allowed back on top of her desk. A student is selected by the teacher to be the judge for the game to determine whether tosses are too high, too hard, etc. If a player talks above a whisper at any time during the game, he must sit down in his chair for the whole game.

Variations: (1) Have players throw with non-dominant hand. (2) Have players catch each toss with only one hand.

BALLOON BALL

Grades: 2–6

Purposes: To promote group coordination
To develop coordination and flexibility

Equipment: One balloon, plus spares

Description: Form two teams. Have students arrange desks in two sections of three or five rows, with opposing sections facing each other. Allow three feet between opposing sections. Team members arrange themselves in a staggered pattern, so that teammates are in every other row on both sides of the court. Players must remain in their seats while they bat the balloon back and forth, trying to hit it into the goal area of the opposing team. To score a point, a team must hit the balloon so that it touches the floor in back of the opposing team; other floor touchings do not count. The fun comes in having members of the opposing team in with your own!

Variations: (1) Use two or three balloons at the same time. (2) Allow team members to switch positions after each goal.

ROUND-TRIP DODGEBALL

Grades: 2–6

Purposes: To promote team cooperation
To improve overall physical fitness
To develop throwing accuracy

Equipment: Several foam rubber balls or balled-up socks

Description: Push desks aside. Divide the class into three equal teams. Two teams form lines facing each other on opposite sides of the room. The third team forms a single-file line in the middle of one end of the room. Place a cone or waste paper basket at the other end of the room. The object is for players in the single-file line to run down to the cone and back without getting hit with a foam rubber ball thrown by the opposing two teams. One point is given for each direction completed successfully. Players run for the cone one at a time; however, the teacher may send another runner shortly after the first has left. After each player from one team has gone, rotate teams.

Variations: (1) Use more or fewer foam rubber balls. (2) Vary throwing style: overhand, underhand, non-dominant arm.

NEWCOMB

Grades: 2–6

Purposes: To develop lead-up skills for volleyball
To improve hand/eye coordination
To promote team cooperation

Equipment: A piece of rope or string
Foam rubber ball or beach ball

Description: Push the desks aside. Divide the class into two equal teams. Stretch a piece of rope across the center of the room. Teams scatter themselves on opposite sides of the net, facing the opposing team. Each player is given a number for serving. The server stands behind the end line and must throw the ball over the net into the opposing team's territory. The opposing team attempts to catch the ball. The ball is thrown back and forth until it drops to the floor. The object of the game is to throw the ball over the net in an attempt to strike an unguarded place on the floor of the opponent's territory. (Rotation and scoring are done according to traditional volleyball rules.)

Variations: (1) Have players throw and catch with non-dominant hand. (2) Allow players to use only one hand to catch. (3) For advanced players, switch to normal volleyball.

BLIND FIND

Grades: 2–6

Purposes: To promote cooperation
To have fun

Equipment: A few blindfolds

Description: Have the children form an oval in the front or back of the room, or push the desks aside and have players form a circle. Two players who are chosen to be *It*, position themselves in the center of the circle. Both center players are then blindfolded. One child is chosen to be the chaser, the other child tries to keep from being tagged. The chaser calls, "Where are you?" or "I need a hint," while the other child answers, "Here I am," or "Try and catch me." The one being chased must move quickly and quietly to avoid being tagged. Guided by voice, the chaser tries to tag the other child. When someone is tagged, he becomes the chaser, and the original chaser chooses someone to take his place. A time limit may also be set to end the game when no one is tagged, in which case both players choose someone to come into the circle. Players forming the circle gently guide blindfolded players and serve to prevent collisions and injuries.

Variations: (1) Play the game with one chaser and two or more children to be chased. (2) Have the children form smaller groups and have several games going at the same time.

BOX BALL

Grades: 2–6

Purposes: To develop quickness and hand/eye coordination
To promote teamwork and cooperation
To increase overall physical fitness

Equipment: Four balls of any type
A large box

Description: Push the desks aside. Divide the group into four equal teams. Each team must number off by ones. Each team forms a line facing the center of the room, which forms a square. To begin the game, the leader calls a number. The player with that number for each team runs to the box in the center of the room, gets the ball, and hands it to the end player on his team. Meanwhile, other players move down to fill the vacant place. The end player hands the ball to the next player; the ball is passed in this manner to the last player on the team who runs and puts it back in the box and goes to the head of the line. The first ball to be put in the box scores one point for that team. The teams may keep their own scores, or a scorekeeper can be assigned. (Each player keeps his original number although his position constantly changes).

Variations: (1) Have players perform a task while they are retrieving and returning the ball (for example; hop all the way, do a crab walk instead of running, skip all the way, etc.). (2) Have players perform a task as they pass the ball down the line (for example; pass the ball behind the back all the way, use the over-under passing technique, squeeze the ball between the knees and pass from player to player in that fashion, etc.).

GO AHEAD, MAKE ME LAUGH

Grades: 2–6

Purposes: To provide a fun and relaxing activity

Equipment: None

Description: Have the group form two teams. The two teams form lines, facing each other. Team one's first person tries to make team two's first person laugh, but team two's player tries to keep a solemn face. Each team member has thirty seconds to make the other team's member laugh. If an individual laughs, she gives up a point to the other team. Repeat the procedure until everyone has had a turn at both tasks.

Variations: (1) By elimination, pick the best clown and solemn face and have a championship round. (2) Have everyone go at the same time rather than individually. (3) Rotate players and play several rounds.

SEVEN-UP

Grades: 2–6

Purposes: To reinforce concepts being studied in a variety of subjects
To have an enjoyable time

Equipment: None

Description: Seven students are selected by the leader to come to the front of the room. Have the rest of the group members place their heads on their desks so that they cannot see, with one arm outstretched and the thumb pointing up. The seven players go around the room and tap the thumbs of seven others, and then line up in front of the room. The group of seven players chosen by the leader says, "Heads-Up Seven-Up." Those who were tapped stand and try to guess which one tapped them. If the tapper is guessed, they exchange places. If the tapper is not guessed, she continues for another round. Others do not indicate which student did the tapping until all have had their chance to guess.

Variations: (1) Start the game with only two people doing the tapping. Each consecutive round, add one person to the game. (2) Play "Task Seven-Up," and require the successful completion of a math or spelling problem in addition to the correct identification of the tapper.

CHUCK IT AND CHECK IT*

Grades: 2–6

Purposes: To promote group cooperation
To develop eye/hand coordination
To have fun

Equipment: One or more foam rubber balls or playground balls (other objects may be used: beanbags, tennis balls, etc.)

Description: One child is chosen to be the thrower. He stands with his back to the group (who are scattered about the play area) and throws the object in the air behind him. The player who receives the object hides it behind his back; to confuse the thrower, the object may be passed from player to player before it is hidden. All players hide their hands behind their backs and shout in unison, "Check It!" The thrower turns around and has three guesses to name the player holding the object. If successful, he is the thrower again; if not, the holder of the object is the new thrower.

Variations: (1) Have one thrower throw two balls, or two throwers throw one ball each. (2) Break children into smaller groups to allow several games to be played at the same time.

---

*Bryant, Rosalie and Oliver, Eloise McLean, *Fun and Fitness Through Elementary Physical Education*, West Nyack, New York: Parker Publishing Company, Inc., 1967.

BLANKETBALL*

Grades: 2–6

Purposes: To promote group cooperation
To enjoy the activity

Equipment: A piece of rope or string
A blanket or sheet
Several foam rubber balls or wads of scratch paper

Description: Push the desks aside. Stretch a rope across the room by tying it to a couple of chairs or desks. Divide the group into two equal teams. The teams scatter themselves on opposite sides of the net, facing each other. One team has a blanket covered with several balls or wads of paper, or a combination of the two. On the leader's signal, the balls are propelled over the net with the blanket. The opposing team gets a point for every ball caught. The serving team gets one point for every ball that hits the ground in bounds. Any ball landing out of bounds is subtracted from the serving team's score. The winner is the team with the most points at the end of a given time period or the one to reach a certain point total.

Variations: (1) Have the receiving team catch the balls with a blanket (towel or sheets held by small groups of players can be used). (2) Vary the number of balls used from just a few to several.

---

*Tillman, Kenneth G. and Toner, Patricia Rizzo, *What Are We Doing in Gym Today?*, West Nyack, New York: Parker Publishing Company, Inc., 1983.

RING ON A STRING

Grades: 2–6

Purposes: To have a great time

Equipment: A piece of string long enough to form a circle accommodating all of the players
A ring large enough to slide along the string

Description: Have players form a circle. Place a ring on the string and tie the ends together. Players sit or stand in a circle, holding the string, palms down. One player acts as the "detective." The players holding the string pass the ring from one to another. The detective in the middle attempts to find the ring; the players in the circle try to deceive him by moving their hands as if passing the ring. If the detective thinks he has found the ring, he points to the hands of the suspected player. If he is correct, the two exchange places. If a detective makes five mistakes, he is discharged, and the last person accused of having the ring takes his place.

Variations: (1) Use more than one ring. (2) Have more than one "detective" in the center.

CLANDESTINE CLOTHESPIN

Grades: 2–6

Purposes: To promote cooperation
To provide for the reinforcement of concepts being taught in a variety of subject areas
To have fun

Equipment: One clothespin

Description: Players can either form a circle or scatter themselves about the room for this activity. Have all players shut their eyes except one person. That person will hide the clothespin on someone in the group. It has to be visible, not under hair or clothing. Once the person has hidden the clothespin, he signals the others to open their eyes and begin looking for the clothespin. If a person sees it, he or she sits down. The last person to see the clothespin hides it the next game.

Variations: Play TASK CLANDESTINE CLOTHESPIN, in which the last player to spot the clothespin must perform a task before the next round (sing a song, solve a problem, tell a joke, skip around the room, etc.).

TABLE-TOP FOOTBALL

Grades: 4–6

Purposes: To develop small motor coordination
To provide a review of addition facts and computation

Equipment: A piece of scratch paper for each pair of players

Description: Players form groups of two and sit on opposite sides of a desk, facing each other. The pair must first construct a football out of the piece of paper. This is done with a triangular folding pattern (the way a flag is folded). The object of the game is to flick the football toward the opponent's side of the desk, and make the ball hang over the edge of the desk without falling off. If a player is successful in flicking the ball so that it hangs over the edge of the desk, she scores a touchdown (6 points), and is allowed to attempt an extra point (1 point). To score an extra point, the player places the football on his own 20 yard line and flicks the ball in the air between the goalposts (hands held in a goal post position by opposing player). After a score, the ball is given to the opposing player for a kick-off. If a player flicks the ball off the end of the desk, the ball is given to the opposing player for the next shot.

Variations: (1) Give each player 3 downs or flicks to move the ball upfield and hang it over the edge of the desk. (2) Allow opposing players to attempt a field goal (3 points—same procedure as an extra point) each time a player flicks the ball off the edge or end of the table, rather than simply changing possession.

POOR MAN'S AIR HOCKEY

Grades: 4–6

Purposes: To improve hand/eye coordination
To have fun

Equipment: A flat round sponge, approximately 3 inches in diameter, will serve as the "puck"
Larger pieces of sponge, jar lids, chalkboard erasers, small boxes or other devices can be used as hand held "hockey sticks"

Description: Two players stand at opposite ends of a table or desk, facing each other. Books are lined up on both sides of the table to form walls that will keep the puck in play. The puck is put into play by dropping it in the center of the table. The object is to hit the puck so that it goes off the other end of the table. One point is scored each time the puck is driven off the opponent's end of the table. If a player lets go of his hockey stick, a point is subtracted from his or her total.

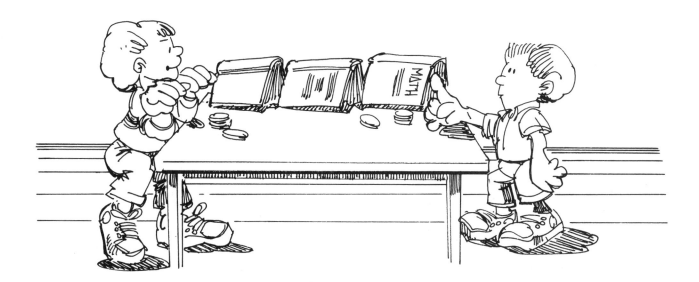

Variations: (1) Have players rotate at specified time intervals so that each person faces every other player; in this version, the player with the greatest point total at the end of the games is the winner. (2) On larger tables, have the players form teams of two or three and play with four or six people at a time.

GROUP JUGGLING

Grades: 4–6

Purposes: To promote group cooperation
To improve hand/eye coordination
To improve throwing accuracy

Equipment: Any objects that can be easily caught such as:
Tennis balls
Foam rubber balls
Balled up socks
Wads of paper

Description: Have the players form circles with about ten people in each group. One person begins by throwing an object to someone across the circle. She, in turn, tosses it to someone across from her, and so on until each person has received a toss. The last person tosses the object back to the starter and thus a pattern has been established. The sequence is repeated and each participant tosses to the same person each time. Then a new object is added (it chases the first object through the pattern) and the fun begins! Next, a third object is introduced into the pattern, then another, until five or more objects are in flight at once. The activity takes concentration and lots of teamwork!

Variations: (1) Have the entire class form one large circle and try the game using longer throws. (2) Use different shapes and sizes of objects when throwing (ping-pong balls, foam rubber footballs, sponges, rubber snakes, etc.).

THE GREAT SHOE STRIP

Grades: 4–6

Purposes: To promote group cooperation
To improve strength and physical fitness

Equipment: None

Description: Have the students form a small circle, pressing tightly together. The group slowly sits down so as not to injure anyone. The object of the game is for players to try to prevent others from removing their shoes (without kicking) while trying to remove as many shoes as is possible from the feet of other players. If a player manages to remove someone's shoe, she is to toss it outside the circle. The winner is the one with one or both shoes on after everyone else has been "shoe stripped." (This game is a good lead-up game for, "Clean Up Your Yard")

Variations: (1) Rather than having students stay in the circle area, allow them to "crab walk" around the room to avoid being "stripped." (2) Have players form teams rather than compete individually.

IT'S A TOSS-UP

Grades: 4–6

Purposes: To increase hand/eye coordination
To improve quickness and reaction time
To promote cooperation

Equipment: Several tennis balls, foam rubber balls, or wads of paper or balled-up rags

Description: Players may remain in or stand near their seats. Divide the group into two to five teams by giving each person a team name (use football or baseball team names, or use vocabulary words from science, social studies, etc.). The leader throws balls in all directions as fast as possible, and players attempt to catch as many balls as they can without leaving their seat or standing position. Point totals can be kept for each team, and the team with the most points at the end of the play period wins.

Variations: (1) Have the players who caught a ball attempt to throw it back into a trash can near the leader to score an additional point for their team. (2) Try a round in which two or three throwers are used to make the game even more challenging. The leader can also put the balls in a bucket or similar container and fling them all at once.

BOP A LOT

Grades: 4–6

Purposes: To promote cooperation
                To improve agility and quickness

Equipment: Several balloons
                 Some hoops or old bicycle tires

Description: Hoops or tires are placed randomly about the play area. Players form pairs and are given a balloon. The object is for players to bat the balloon back and forth, each player hitting the balloon once per turn, while trying to score a point. Points are scored when one player picks up a hoop, while the other one bats the balloon through it, and the hoop is placed back on the floor. Players continue on to the next hoop while keeping the balloon in the air, and the process is repeated. See how many points can be scored by the entire group in a certain amount of time, or have pairs keep individual scores.

Variations: (1) Have players pass through the hoop each time as well as the balloons. (2) Play a round with groups of three, four, or five. (3) Play a round in which teams can attempt to block other teams' pursuit for points while they are attempting to score.

CLASSROOM VOLLEYBALL

Grades: 4–6

Purposes: To improve hand/eye coordination, quickness and agility
To practice volley ball lead-up skills
To promote team cooperation

Equipment: A piece of string or rope
A large foam rubber ball

Description: Stretch a piece of rope across the center of the classroom. This game may be played with the desks pushed aside, or children can play while sitting on top of desks. Divide the group into two equal teams. Teams space themselves on opposite sides of the rope, facing each other. The large foam rubber ball is served into play by one team, and modified volleyball rules apply throughout the game. The game can be played to a given point total, or a time limit may be set. Mark boundaries with chalk, tape, or classroom furniture.

Variations: (1) The game can be played while standing, sitting on the floor, or sitting on desk tops. (2) Have three teams which rotate in and out each time the serving team loses a point. (3) Have players catch and throw the ball back and forth rather than hitting it.

INVENT A SPORT

Grades: 4–6

Purposes: To encourage students to use creative thinking and reasoning skills
To provide exercise for overall physical fitness

Equipment: Miscellaneous classroom objects

Description: Have players form groups of three to five. Pass out one or more objects to each team. The leader explains that each group will be given a certain amount of time to make up a game, sport, or activity which can be played by all members of the entire group, using only the object or objects they are given. Teams are responsible for inventing, organizing and formulating the rules for their games. After a given number of minutes call the groups back together and have each team explain and lead their new games. Use the most popular games in future indoor physical education sessions.

Variations: (1) Play "Silent Invent a Sport" in which teams must explain their new games with gestures and motions only—no oral instructions! (2) Allow groups to choose their own objects and play another round.

PINBALL SOCCER

Grades: 4–6

Purposes: To improve foot/eye coordination
             To provide practice of lead-up skills for soccer

Equipment: One or more foam rubber or playground balls

Description: Divide the group into two equal teams. Place a chair or desk at each end of the room to serve as the goals. Mark a zone around the goals to indicate that players are not allowed in, since the game is played with no goalies. Players from both teams scatter about the play area in offensive and defensive positions. To begin the game, the ball is placed in the center of the room, and one team kicks off. The object is to pass the ball from player to player between chair and desk legs and score by kicking it through the goal at the far end of the room. Players must stay in their zones during the action to avoid crowding. The ball is always in play, since there are no out of bounds areas. Action only stops after a goal is scored, at which time the ball is placed in the center of the room and the team previously scored upon puts the ball in play and the game continues.

Variations: (1) To involve more players, play with three balls at the same time by placing one in the center and one on each side of the room to start. (2) After each goal is scored, have players change positions to allow everyone a chance to play defensively as well as offensively.

SPORTS THEATRE

Grades: 4–6

Purposes: To promote creativity and expression
To promote cooperation
To provide exercise for overall physical fitness

Equipment: None

Description: Have players form groups of three to six. Instruct groups to meet for a few minutes to develop a skit which incorporates some type of strenuous exercise. Groups may act out portions of sporting events, or they may include some element of sport or exercise in any type of setting or situation. Allow plenty of freedom, and let students have fun with the activity, while making sure they include some sort of vigorous movement in their presentations.

Variations: (1) Have students repeat the activity using pantomime as the method of expression. (2) Switch from sports to other forms of exercise (skits involving hard work, rowing in a life boat, running from bears, etc.).

III
MARVELOUS
MOVEMENT
GAMES

HOT BALL

Grades: K–2

Purposes: To increase flexibility
To improve coordination and quickness

Equipment: One or more utility balls.

Description: Push desks aside. Have children sit on the floor in a circle. One child puts his hand over the ball, heats it red hot, and then rolls it toward the center. To keep the ball hot, it must be on the move all the time. The children do this by batting it with their hands as soon as it comes their way. Anyone failing to bat the ball or allowing the ball to stop has to get up and run, hop or skip around the circle once.

Variations: (1) Use more than one ball. (2) Have students form smaller groups and play several games at the same time.

FROG MAN

Grades: K–2

Purposes: To increase flexibility
To improve physical fitness

Description: One child is chosen to be the "Frog Man." His or her chair is taken away, or if the room has desks, a book is placed on the desk to indicate it is not to be used. The same thing is done with other vacant seats. Frog Man comes to the front of the room and stoops down like a frog. Five or more children are chosen to form a circle around the Frog Man. They join hands and walk or skip around the Frog Man saying, "Frog Man, Frog Man, in the sea." They continue going around the Frog Man chanting as they go, until the Frog Man jumps up and starts to run to a vacant seat. The children in the circle let go of hands and run back to their seats. The one left without a seat becomes the new Frog Man.

Variations: Have the entire class form the circle around all of the desks, with the Frog Man in the center of the room.

CIRCLE STRIDE BALL

Grades: K–4

Purposes: To improve coordination
To increase flexibility
To provide exercise for overall fitness

Equipment: One or more playground or foam rubber balls

Description: Move desks aside. Have players form a circle and take a stride position with feet touching. One player is in the center of the circle. She attempts to bat or roll the ball out of the circle between the feet of any player. If the center person is successful, the player between whose feet the ball passed becomes "It." Players on the circle use their hands to stop the ball, and then return it to the center.

Variations: 1) Have more than one player in the center. 2) Use more than one ball.

YARN BALL VOLLEYBALL

Grades: K–4

Purposes: To promote team cooperation
To provide skills for volleyball
To improve hand eye coordination

Equipment: One yarn ball or foam rubber ball
A piece of rope or string.

Description: Push desks aside. Stretch a rope across an open space and tie each end to a chair. Have children form two teams, and scatter out covering the playing area in sitting position. Children then try to throw and catch over the rope. Points may be scored when the ball touches the ground or goes under the net. You may just want to set a time limit instead of keeping score.

Variations: Have students assume a kneeling position.

CLOWN SPONGE BALLS

Grades: K–4

Purposes: To improve throwing skills and hand/eye coordination
To provide lead-up skills for baseball
To improve number identification and addition skills

Equipment: Several sponges or foam rubber balls

Description: Draw four large clowns on the blackboard. Divide the class into four teams. Children stand 7 to 10 feet from the clown. Players throw a moist sponge or foam rubber ball, and try to hit the clown. Different areas of the clown are worth certain points. Points are accumulated by teams as members hit certain areas of the clown. Each child throws once and goes to the end of the line. A point total or time limit may be set to end the game. A student or an aide may be assigned to judge "liners" and to keep score.

Variations: Have players throw with non-dominant hand.

DROP AND GO

Grades: K–4

Purposes: To develop physical fitness
To have fun

Equipment: None

Description: All of the children except one sit at their desks with their heads resting on one arm as though sleeping, with eyes closed, and with one hand outstretched. One child is chosen to be "It." The child chosen to be It carries an object (piece of chalk, eraser, coin, etc.) as he walks quietly about the room and drops the object into the open hand of a child. The child jumps up from his seat and chases It, who is safe only when he reaches his seat. If It reaches his seat without being caught, he may choose to be It again. Otherwise, the child who caught him becomes the new It.

Variations: Have two or more children be It at the same time, each dropping objects into the hands of other children simultaneously.

CATCH BASKET

Grades: K–4

Purposes: To develop number identification and addition skills
To improve hand/eye coordination

Equipment: Two or more beanbags or wads of scrap paper

Description: Divide the class into two equal teams. Place each team in a semicircle along either side of the room. Place a wastebasket on a center desk, with a child standing near it. Alternating from side to side each child, in turn, tries to throw the beanbag or paper wad into the basket. The center monitor returns the bag or paper to the next thrower. Each time the bag goes into the basket, it scores two points. At the end of a given time, the team with the most points wins. Change the center monitor from time to time.

Variations: (1) Change the point value for each shot to 3,4,5 etc., for practice in adding different numbers. (2) Have children throw with non-dominant hand. (3) Break into smaller groups and have several games going at once. (4) If each player has a beanbag or paper wad, have all the members of a team throw at the same time. (5) Give bonus points for trick shots (5 points for behind the back, 10 points for between the legs).

BIRD CATCHER

Grades: K–4

Purposes: To promote physical fitness
To provide for the introduction or reinforcement of concepts from various subjects
To promote cooperation and sportsmanship

Equipment: None

Description: Push the desks aside. The children stand behind a goal line in an area designated as the "forest." Each child chooses the name of a bird (or the teacher may assign a bird name to each child). Several children may have the same bird name. The "Birdcatcher" stands in the area between the forest and the birds' nest. Birdcatcher calls, "Robins fly" (or eagles, sparrows, or whatever he chooses). The children whose bird name is called run to the nest. Any child caught is sent to the Bird Cage. After the Birdcatcher has called several bird names, he may call, "Birds fly" and all remaining birds in the forest must run to the nest. When all have run, the Birdcatcher chooses a new Birdcatcher from those who reached the nest safely; the birds go back to the forest and the game starts again.

Variations: (1) Specify certain body parts that the "Birdcatcher" must tag on the birds (feet, elbows, knees, etc.). (2) Use different types of animals, plants, or names of items which reinforce topics being studied in science, reading or social studies.

SEAT TAG

Grades: K–4

Purposes: To improve overall physical fitness
To develop quickness and agility

Equipment: None

Description: Children remain in their seats to begin the game. A runner and a tagger are chosen. On the leader's command, the tagger chases the runner. At any time, a runner may prevent himself from being tagged by sitting in the seat of another player. The person with whom he sits becomes the new tagger, and the former tagger becomes the runner. If a runner is tagged while running, he becomes the tagger and the tagger becomes the runner.

Variations: (1) Assign certain body parts to be tagged (knees, elbows, feet, etc.). (2) Have children skip or hop rather than run.

GOOD MORNING

Grades: K–4

Purposes: To provide exercise for overall physical fitness

Equipment: None

Description: Arrange the desks to allow the children to form a large circle. The children stand in a circle facing the center while one who is "It" walks or runs around the outside of the circle and touches someone on the back. The two then run in opposite directions. Upon meeting at the other side, they stop and say, "Good morning," and shake hands. Then they both race for the vacant place. The first one there wins and is It for the next turn. Players failing to stop and say, "Good morning," and shake hands are eliminated from the game for a set number of turns.

Variations: SLAP JACK—Players form a circle, standing with hands behind, palms up. "It" runs around the circle and slaps the palms of another player. The player who was slapped chases It and tries to tag him before he can reach the vacant spot.

SNOWSHOE RACE

Grades: K–6

Purposes: To promote group cooperation
To increase strength and fitness

Equipment: Several paper plates, box lids, or sheets of newspaper.

Description: Push desks aside. Form teams of six to ten children. The teams line up in a single-file line at one end of the room. Place one chair for each team at the other end of the room. At the signal, the first players put their feet on the "snowshoes" and shuffle along the floor. Each team member races across the room, around the chair, and back. Then a teammate puts on the snowshoes and repeats the journey. The first team to finish is the winner.

Variation: Have students shuffle backwards.

ROLLERBALL

Grades: K–6

Purposes: To increase leg strength and flexibility
To promote physical fitness
To improve quickness and coordination

Equipment: One or more foam rubber or playground balls

Description: Push desks aside. Have the players form a circle and choose someone to be in the middle. Players around the circle try to *roll* the ball(s) to hit the feet of people in the middle. When a player is hit, she changes places with the player that hit her, and the game continues.

Variations: (1) Use more than one ball. (2) Have two, three, or four players in the middle of the circle. (3) Play a game with two teams; one team will form the circle and the other team will be inside. In this version, when players are hit, they join the circle and the last player inside wins.

TOP HOP

Grades: K–6

Purposes: To improve overall fitness
To develop quickness

Equipment: A top

Description: Have the players sit in a circle. One player comes forward and gives the top a spin. The spinner attempts to run around the circle a set number of times before the top falls over. The spinner chooses someone else to spin the top, and the process is repeated.

Variations: (1) Change the task to be completed. Have the players attempt to dribble a ball while running around the circle, hop on one leg, dribble a foam rubber soccer ball around the circle, etc. (2) To involve more players, allow the ones sitting in the circle to roll a large marble or tennis ball across the circle to try to knock the top over before the spinner can complete the task.

CLASSROOM BOWLING

Grades: K–6

Purposes: To improve coordination and flexibility
To develop lead-up skills for bowling
To review addition facts and computation

Equipment: Several balls (volleyballs, softballs, playground balls, or foam rubber balls)

Description: Arrange the classroom to allow for several "alleys." Divide the group into teams of four. Chairs or desks are placed about twenty feet from the throwing line. Each player attempts to roll the ball in between the legs of the chair or desk. If the ball goes through without touching the legs, two points are scored. If the ball hits a leg and then goes through, score one point. The game can be played individually or in teams of two. Have children play to a given point total, or set a time limit on the game.

Variations: (1) Have players bowl with non-dominant hand. (2) Play a round with only trick shots allowed (between the legs, bent over, with back to the chair, between the legs, etc.).

RING FLING

Grades: K–6

Purposes: To increase hand/eye coordination

Equipment: Several rings made from plastic lids or paper plates with the center cut out or lengths of rope taped together to form a circle

Description: Have players form groups of three to five. Each group turns a chair upside down and stands a few feet away. The object is for players to ring one of the chair legs as many times as they can, given an equal number of throws. The player with the most successful tosses wins. The game can be played in teams of two or three.

Variations: (1) Have players use trick throws or throw from a greater distance. (2) Have players attempt throws using their non-dominant hand.

CLASSROOM LIMBO

Grades: K–6

Purposes: To increase flexibility
To improve balance

Equipment: A piece of string, yarn, rope, or a yardstick

Description: Clear a small space for the Limbo area. Two students are chosen to hold the ends of the string, rope, or other chosen material. The holders stand several feet apart while holding the string level at about shoulder height. The first player leans backward while shuffling under the Limbo line. Each player goes under the line in the same fashion at the first height. After everyone has gone at the first height, the line is lowered and the process is repeated. Allow all players to participate at each level. The winner is the one who can shuffle under the line without touching it or falling to the floor at the lowest height.

Variations: (1) Have players try to go under in pairs while holding hands. (2) Play an appropriate record or tape during the activity to add to the excitement.

EXCHANGE TAG

Grades: 2–4

Purposes: To provide exercise for overall fitness
To have fun

Equipment: None

Description: Choose one child to be *It,* and have him stand in front of the room. The teacher calls the names of any two children who, as soon as their names are called, exchange seats. The one who is It tries to tag one of them before they reach each other's seat. The one who is seated first becomes It for the next round. If It tags a player before he is seated, he may choose to be It again.

Variations: (1) Call three or more names on some rounds. (2) Have more than one child be It.

PIN GUARD

Grades: 2–6

Purposes: To improve hand/eye coordination
To enhance throwing skills
To increase flexibility

Equipment: One or more foam rubber balls
One plastic bowling pin, cone, or similar object

Description: Push desks aside. Have children form a circle, with one child in the center. An object is placed in the center of a smaller circle (drawn with chalk line or use tape) and is guarded by the center child, who must stay outside the smaller circle. Those in the large circle roll or throw a foam rubber ball trying to hit the object in the center. If a player knocks the object over, he or she changes places with the guard. The guard must bat or kick the ball away from the object.

Variations: (1) Have more than one guard. (2) Use more than one ball.

SOCCER DODGEBALL

Grades: 2–6

Purposes: To improve foot/eye coordination
To develop quickness
To develop lead-up skills for soccer

Equipment: One or more foam rubber balls

Description: Push chairs aside. Players stand one pace apart in a circle, facing inward, except for one player who goes into the center of the circle. The object of the game is to hit the player in the middle by kicking the ball. The player in the middle dodges the ball. When hit, the player in the middle is replaced by the person who kicked the ball. Count only hits that land below the waist.

Variations: (1) Use more than one ball. (2) Have more than one person in the middle. (3) Have players kick with non-dominant foot. (4) Have players squat and bat the ball with their hands.

BROOM HOCKEY

Grades: 2–6

Purposes: To improve overall physical fitness
To develop coordination and agility

Equipment: Two or more brooms or rolled up magazines
One or more foam rubber or playground balls

Description: Push desks aside. Put one desk at each end of the room. A shot between the legs of the desk is a goal. Divide the group into two teams and have each team's players count off by numbers. Each team will then stand behind the goal with one person (or more, depending on the number of brooms) holding the broom. The foam rubber ball is placed in the middle of the room. A number (or numbers) is called out and each team member with that number must grab a broom and try to get the ball into the opposing team's goal.

Variations: (1) At times call more than one number. (2) Allow teammates to line up at the edge of the playing area and assist their players by kicking the ball to them when it is hit out of bounds.

SPONGE BASEBALL

Grades: 2–6

Purposes: To develop hand/eye coordination and throwing accuracy
To practice lead-up skills for baseball

Equipment: Several sponges or foam rubber balls

Description: Draw a baseball diamond on the chalkboard with designated areas and appropriate labels. Form two teams. Have the players stand 10 to 15 feet away from the target. Each team member gets a turn to throw a moist sponge or foam ball at it; her base hit, out, or ball is recorded according to the wet spot on the chalkboard. If a player should miss the target completely she may have another chance. A scorekeeper keeps track of players on bases, scoring and outs. When a team has made three outs, the other team is "up to bat." You may also want to appoint an umpire to make calls on "liners."

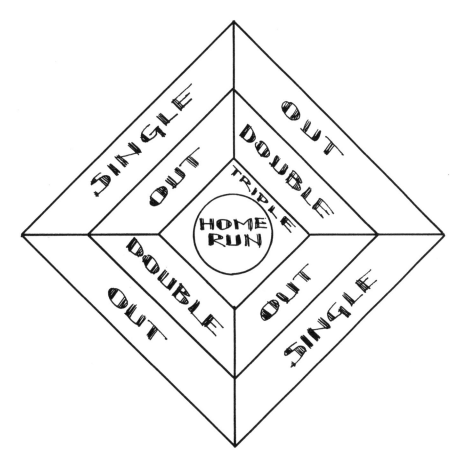

Variations: (1) Draw several diagrams on the board and have several smaller teams playing at the same time. (2) Have players throw with their non-dominant hand.

PICK AND POW*

Grades: 2–6

Purposes: To improve overall physical fitness
To develop coordination and agility
To improve throwing skills

Equipment: One foam rubber ball
Any object such as a bowling pin, eraser, beanbag, etc.

Description: Push the desks aside. Have the group form two equal teams. Teams line up on opposite ends of the room, facing each other. Place a ball and an object at the center of the playing area, about six feet apart. Designate a base area at opposing ends of the team's lines. The game begins when the player on the base of team A says to his opponent (the runner at the opposite end of the B team), "Go for it!" On this signal, both players run toward the ball and pin. The B player picks up the pin and tries to return to his base before the A player can throw the ball and hit him (below the head). Whichever player is successful scores one point for his team. After each has a turn, he goes to the opposite end of his own line. Players on each team shift one position toward their base and the game continues. When each person has run, change the roles of the teams. The winner is the team with the most points at the end of a given time period.

Variations: (1) Change the distance between the ball and object. (2) Have players throw with non-dominant hand. (3) Assign certain body parts to be hit on some rounds (legs, feet, arms, etc.).

---

*Bryant, Rosalie and Oliver, Eloise McLean, *Complete Elementary Physical Education Guide,* West Nyack, New York: Parker Publishing Company, Inc., 1974.

CHANGING SEATS

Grades: 2–6

Purposes: To provide exercise for overall physical fitness

Equipment: None

Description: All players except one are seated. The extra player is the leader. Push extra seats aside, making sure that players outnumber available seats by one. Have the leader assign each player the name of one of four different fruits, vegetables, animals, etc. The leader calls out one of the group names and the players assigned to that group must switch places. While seats are being exchanged, the leader scrambles to reach an empty chair. The player left standing when all the seats are taken becomes the next leader.

Variations: (1) The leader may call out more than one group name during each round, or the leader may call out, "Everyone switch," in which case all the players exchange seats. (2) Play the game with players in a circle with chairs facing the center.

CRAZY CHASE

Grades: 2–6

Purposes: To improve physical fitness
To develop coordination and agility

Equipment: One ball of any type

Description: Push the desks aside. Have children stand in a circle fairly close together and facing in. One player stands outside the circle. The ball is given to a circle player and is passed from player to player or thrown across to an opposite player. The object is for the outside player to tag a circle player while he has the ball in his hands. When the outside player is successful in tagging a player, he changes places with him. If a circle player drops the ball, he becomes the tagger, and the former tagger takes his place.

Variations: (1) Allow only one-handed throws and catches. (2) Have children use a bounce pass for each exchange rather than a toss. (3) Use two outside players and one ball, or two outside players and two balls. (4) Have the tagger move to the inside of the circle.

CIRCLE KICK

Grades: 2–6

Purposes: To provide practice of lead-up skills for soccer
To promote teamwork and group cooperation
To improve overall physical fitness

Equipment: One or more foam rubber balls

Description: Push the desks aside. Divide the group into two teams. One team is lined up around one half of the circle and the other on the opposite side. The ball is put into play by one team kicking it toward the opposing team. Points are scored when the ball is kicked between the legs of the opposing players; but when the ball is kicked above the shoulder level of any player, the team opposite the kicker scores a point. When the ball is kicked by a player through the legs of his own team, the opposing team scores a point.

Variations: (1) Have players throw the ball rather than kick it. (2) Have players kick with non-dominant foot, or throw with non-dominant hand. (3) Use more than one ball.

TRASH CAN B-BALL

Grades: 2–6

Purposes: To improve hand/eye coordination
To practice lead-up skills for basketball

Equipment: A couple of trash cans
Two large foam rubber balls or playground balls

Description: Divide the group into two teams and assign a trash can to each team. Place the two empty trash cans about ten feet apart. Make a foul line with masking tape at the appropriate distance for the age level of the group. Each team member takes one shot at the "basket" and then goes to the end of the line. The team with the most points made after all team members have shot wins that round. Scoring goes as follows:

1. If the ball hits the wall (backboard) or edge of can (rim) and then goes in, score two points.
2. If the ball lands in the "basket" without touching anything (swish), score five points.
3. If a player steps on, or crosses the foul line after a shot, the points do not count.

Variations: (1) Make two foul lines, and allow brave players to shoot from the greater distance for more points. (2) Break the group into smaller teams and have several teams shooting at the same time. (3) Have players bounce the ball into the "basket" rather than shooting it through the air. (4) Have players shoot with non-dominant hand. (5) Play a round with only trick shots allowed (between the legs, over the head with back to the "basket," behind the back, etc.).

TOO HOT TO HANDLE

Grades: 2–6

Purposes: To improve quickness and hand/eye coordination
To increase overall physical fitness

Equipment: One or more foam rubber balls or playground balls

Description: Push the desks aside. Have players form a circle, facing in, standing or sitting. The ball is thrown from one player to another in a random pattern until "Too Hot to Handle" is called by the leader or child appointed for the purpose. The player holding the ball when "Too Hot to Handle" is called must perform a task: hop, skip, or run around the circle; recite a math fact; read a paragraph. Players who drop the ball or make a bad pass may also be asked to perform a predetermined task.

Variations: (1) Have players use only one hand to throw and catch. (2) Use two, or even three balls at the same time.

PICK IT QUICK

Grades: 2–6

Purposes: To develop quickness and agility
To exercise and increase physical fitness

Equipment: A rag, handkerchief, sock, or any piece of material

Description: Push the desks aside. Divide the group into two equal teams. Each team stands in a straight line facing the other team, which is about ten feet away. One team numbers off from one end of the line, while the other team numbers off from the other end. Place the object in the center of the playing area. The leader calls a number, for example 4. The number 4 player from each line runs to the object. Each player tries to snatch the object and take it back to his place in line without being tagged by his opponent. Each may make several fake attempts to snatch the object before actually picking it up to run with it. The scoring goes as follows: if the player from Team 1 snatches the object and reaches his goal without being tagged, he scores two points for his team, if his opponent tags him, one point is scored for Team II. Play up to a given point total, or set a time limit on the game.

Variations: (1) Call two numbers instead of just one. (2) Use an old bicycle tire for the object in the center. In this version, the same rules apply except when both players grab the tire, in which case the winner is the one that can tug the opponent across his team's line.

BOP YOUR BUDDY

Grades: 2–6

Purposes: To improve overall physical fitness
To have a great time

Equipment: An old stocking or sock stuffed with cotton, rags, or newspaper.

Description: Push the desks into the center of the room, or push them aside. Have the children form a circle, looking straight ahead with their hands behind them. One child is chosen to be the "Bopper," and goes around the outside of the circle with the bopping apparatus. He lays it in some player's hands, and runs around the circle to the vacant spot. The one who received the bopping apparatus runs after him and bops him as many times as she can before the opponent can reach the vacant spot in the circle. The new Bopper begins the procedure again.

Variations: (1) Break the group into three or four circles to allow more player interaction. (2) Have the person being chased make two or three trips around the circle to allow more bopping time.

BIFF OR BE BIFFED*

Grades: 2–6

Purposes: To improve overall physical fitness
To develop quickness and agility
To improve throwing skills

Equipment: Two or more foam rubber balls

Description: Push the desks aside. Divide the group into two equal teams. The teams form a circle, each on its own half of a dividing line. Place one ball on each side of the dividing line near the center of the circle. Each member of each team is given a number. The leader calls a number and one player from each team runs to pick up a ball and tries to hit his opponent before being hit. Other players can get a loose ball and return it to their center player, but cannot hit the opposing center player themselves. The first center player to hit his opponent scores a point for his team. Players must stay in their half of the circle.

Variations: (1) Have four or six balls in the center and call two or three numbers on the same round. (2) Have players throw with non-dominant hand. (3) Assign certain body parts to be hit: feet, knees, hands, etc.

---

*Tillman, Kenneth G., and Toner, Patricia Rizzo, *What Are We Doing in Gym Today?*, West Nyack, New York: Parker Publishing Company, Inc., 1983.

QUICK FLICK

Grades: 2–6

Purposes: To improve coordination, flexibility and agility
To increase overall physical fitness

Equipment: One or two large foam rubber balls or playground balls

Description: Push the desks aside. Have the players form a circle with one person in the middle. The ball is given to one player, who quickly tosses it to someone else. The ball is passed quickly from player to player while the person in the middle attempts to tag someone while she has the ball. If a player is tagged with the ball, she must trade places with the person in the middle. If a player drops the ball when attempting to catch it, she must trade places with the center person.

Variations: (1) Have two players in the middle of the circle. (2) Play with two balls instead of using only one. (3) Have players make one-handed catches only. (4) Leave the desks in place, and have the children play the game while sitting on top of their desks.

FOUR CORNERS SOCCER

Grades: 2–6

Purposes: To improve foot/eye coordination
                To practice lead-up skills for soccer
                To promote teamwork and group cooperation

Equipment: A foam rubber ball (a wad of paper or a crushed milk carton will do)

Description: Push desks aside. Have the players form two equal teams. Teams form lines at opposite ends of the room, facing each other. The leader begins the action by calling, "Corners," and throwing the ball into the center of the room. When the ball is thrown, players on the ends of each team's line run to the center of the room and attempt to control the ball. Each team tries to move the ball toward the opposing goal line and score. All members of each team are goalies when not involved in field play. A point is scored when one team kicks a goal (below shoulder level) through the opposing team's goal line. After a goal is scored, field players go back to the middle of their line, and all players shift one space in either direction toward the ends of the lines. If one team manages to stop a scoring attempt and one of the goalies controls the ball, the ball goes back to the leader and new field players participate in the next round. The winner is the team that reaches a certain point total first, or the team with the most points after a given time period. (Standard soccer rules apply throughout the game.)

Variations: (1) The leader may call, "doubles" or "triples,"which means that four or six players from each team will run to the center. (2) Have players bat the ball with their hands rather than using their feet. (3) Play the game with classroom furniture in place. In this version, players can scatter about the room and goals can be scored between desk legs.

PUCK PUSH

Grades: 2–6

Purposes: To improve coordination
To develop touch and finesse

Equipment: One pusher (yardstick with popsicle sticks or rulers taped on to form a Y, an old broom with the middle bristles cut out, or players may push the pucks by hand) for each group of four players
Each player will also need some type of puck (poker chips glued together, crushed milk carton, jar lid, etc.)

Description: Arrange the desks to allow for wide aisles. Have players form teams of four and position themselves at opposite ends of the aisle from each other. Each team needs to mark a scoring zone in some fashion (draw a scoring box with chalk, mark a square with tape, place a piece of scratch paper on the floor, etc.). Using the pusher, players give the puck a shove toward the scoring zone. A puck that ends up inside the scoring zone makes a point for the team. After all four players have taken a turn, the opposing four take their turns, and the game continues. The team with the most points at the end of the time period wins.

Variations: (1) Play "Knock 'Em Puck Push," in which two players from each team are at opposite ends of the aisle, leaving two players from each team at the same end. In this version, players alternate shots and try to knock opponents out of scoring position as well as end up in the scoring zone. (2) Play a round where any puck touching the line is worth one point, while pucks that end up inside the scoring zone count for five points.

INVISIBLE SPORTS

Grades: 2–6

Purposes: To provide exercise for overall physical fitness
To increase flexibility
To promote group cooperation

Equipment: None

Description: Have players scatter about the playing area to allow freedom of movement. Begin by asking several players to announce their favorite sport. The leader may also want to suggest other sports not mentioned by students. The leader gives the signal for players to begin, and players pretend to play their favorite sport using invisible equipment. Whether it be tennis, swimming, roller skating, or any other sport, each player pretends to be engaged in his favorite sport. Soon there will be a room full of active participants in various "invisible sports."

Variations: (1) The leader can blow a whistle and have players "freeze" to capture people in funny poses and allow all players to see what others are doing. (2) Have players of common sports form groups and play together. (3) Have players create the action in slow motion.

INDOOR OLYMPICS

Grades: 2–6

Purposes: To improve overall physical fitness
To increase flexibility
To increase strength
To improve coordination and agility

Equipment: A few straws, cotton balls or wads of paper
Some paper plates
Several books

Description: Set up several stations consisting of indoor track events. Examples of events are:
1. Javelin—Use straws from the lunchroom.
2. Shot Put—Use a cotton ball from the nurse's office.
3. Discus—Use a paper plate.
4. Low, Low Hurdles—Pile up a few books and have runners sprint back and forth ten times, jumping the hurdle each time while someone times them.
5. High Jump—Use a pile of books.
6. Standing Long Jump—Use a yardstick to measure distance jumped.
Other events may be added to the program. Establish a rotation system and have each player participate in some or all of the events. This could be used as a week-long activity.

Variations: (1) Have the students suggest new events and schedule another Indoor Olympics. (2) Challenge another class to a dual indoor track meet.

YES, YOU CAN

Grades: 2–6

Purposes: To improve hand/eye coordination
To improve throwing technique and accuracy

Equipment: One or more tin cans
A few balls

Description: Attach a can (open at both ends) to the ceiling of the room, or mount it on a wall. Have players form teams of five to eight players. Teams line up at the back of the room in relay fashion. On the signal to start, each team passes a ball from player to player to the back of the line and then back up to the front. When the player at the front of the line receives the ball, she/he runs up to the can and tries to throw the ball through it. After one, two, or three tries, or until successful, s/he picks up the ball and runs back to his/her team and the process is repeated until one team reaches a predetermined point total.

Variations: (1) Suspend four or five cans and have teams throw back and forth to each other, attempting to toss the ball through the can. The first team to reach a certain number wins. (2) Change the way the ball is to be passed up and down the line in the relay version (under the leg, over and under, etc.).

NERVOUS WRECK

Grades 4–6

Purposes: To develop quickness and concentration
To improve coordination

Equipment: One or more foam rubber balls (or playground balls)

Description: Have class form a circle after pushing the desks aside. One player stands in the center of the circle holding a ball. All players in the circle must clasp their hands behind their backs. The object of the game is for each circle player to catch the ball if the player with the ball throws it in their direction, but not to move either hand in the event that the thrower pretends to toss the ball but does not release it. When a player errors (misses a tossed ball or moves his hand(s) from behind him when thrower pretends to toss ball but does not release it), he must turn his back to the group until another player errors, whereupon he may turn back. The teacher may want to appoint one student referee to judge close calls. Allow everyone a chance to be the thrower.

Variations: (1) Have thrower bounce tosses rather than throw directly at circle players. (2) Form several circles and have more than one game going at a time. (3) Have more than one player in the center of the circle.

HIT

Grades: 4–6

Purposes: To improve throwing skills
To enhance overall physical fitness

Equipment: One or more foam rubber balls

Description: One student is selected to be "It." He/she stands in the center of the room and throws the ball into the air. All players must change seats when the ball goes up in the air, and continue changing as long as the ball remains up in the air. The person chosen as "It" catches the ball and throws it, attempting to hit a player out of a seat. If he/she does this, the player hit becomes "It." If the player is missed the game starts again with the original "It."

Variations: (1) Have two, three, or four players be "It" at the same time (in this variation, have throwers stand in corners of the room). (2) Have "It" or "Its" throw with non-dominant hand. (3) If more time is needed for runners, have throwers let the ball hit the ground and come to a stop before throwing.

GIVE ME TEN*

Grades: 4–6

Purposes: To improve quickness and agility
To have a great time

Equipment: None

Description: Push the desks aside or make wide aisles. Divide the group into two equal teams. The teams stand at opposite ends of the room, in line, facing each other. One team calls the name of an opposing player and says, ''Karl, Karl, where've you been, come on over and give me ten.'' While Karl runs over, the opposing team members extend both hands, palms up, side by side. With a downward movement, Karl slaps each set of hands in turn. When he slaps the hands of a player with a downward and upward movement, the player chases him home. If caught, Karl becomes a member of the opposing team. If not caught, Karl goes back to join his original team. Then, the other team calls the name of a player, and the game continues with the teams alternating turns. The winning team is the one to get all players on its side or have more players at the end of a given time period.

Variations: (1) Play a round in which the chaser switches teams if he does not tag the other player. (2) Have players hop, do crab walk, etc., instead of run.

---

*Bryant, Rosalie and Oliver, Eloise McLean, *Complete Elementary Physical Education Guide,* West Nyack, New York: Parker Publishing Company, Inc., 1974.

IV
AEROBIC
ACTIVITIES

SUPERMAN (OR SUPERWOMAN)

Grades: K–2

Purposes: To promote cooperation
To develop physical fitness

Equipment: None

Description: Choose one child to be Superman. He stands and says, "Who wants to go with me?" Those who do say, "I do," and fall in line behind him. Superman leads the rest of the group anywhere within a designated area. They must follow him and do everything he does. Suddenly he calls, "Superman!" and all run back to their seats. The one who first gets back in his own seat becomes the next Superman.

Variations: (1) Require Superman to walk backwards as he leads the group. (2) Play music and have the leader begin "seat scramble" by turning off the music.

BASE CHASE

Grades: K–4

Purposes: To promote physical fitness
To improve quickness and agility

Equipment: A home base for each player (piece of linoleum, carpet sample, chalk mark, piece of scrap paper, or piece of newspaper)

Description: Push the desks aside, or play with the room arranged as it is. Start with each player occupying his own home base. One of the children is selected to be the tagger. When the tagger calls, "Go," and leaves his base, all others must leave their base and seek a new one. The tagger attempts to tag one of the players while they are seeking a new base. Players must move farther than one base each round. No two players may occupy the same base at the same time. The person who is tagged becomes the tagger for the next round.

Variations: (1) Have children hop from base to base instead of running. (2) Have two taggers at the same time.

PICK-POCKET TAG

Grades: K–6

Purposes: To increase quickness and agility
To improve balance

Equipment: A scrap of material or piece of paper

Description: Players scatter about the play area. One person is chosen to be *It*, and is given a scrap of material to stuff into his back pocket, leaving the majority of the material exposed. The object is for players to pick It's pocket without being tagged. If a player picks a pocket without being tagged, he indicates a task to be performed by *It* (push-ups, solve a math problem, jump high ten times, etc.). If *It* tags someone before the scrap of material is snatched from his pocket, the two exchange places and the game continues.

Variations: (1) Play the game with two or three *Its* at the same time. (2) Play the game with "It" blindfolded.

CLASSROOM AEROBICS

Grades: K–6

Purposes: To increase strength and endurance
To improve flexibility

Equipment: A record or tape player

Description: Have players spread out and find a space large enough to allow freedom of movement. Instruct participants to follow, to the best of their ability, all the movements made by the leader. Turn on a popular record or tape, and begin leading the group in stretching exercises, calisthenics, and various aerobic movements. Begin with a slow, warm-up pace and build up to a vigorous level of activity toward the end of the session. This can be used as a beginning activity for many or all indoor P.E. sessions.

Variations: (1) Allow students to take over as leaders to add variety and enthusiasm to the activity. (2) Invite a local aerobics instructor to lead the class once in a while to stimulate interest.

BALLOON BURST

Grades: K–6

Purposes: To increase overall fitness and agility
To have fun

Equipment: Several balloons
Some string or twine

Description: Each player is given two balloons to be inflated and tied around each ankle with a piece of string. The object of the game is to burst other players' balloons while protecting one's own balloons. Players may only stomp balloons with their feet, no hands allowed. The winner is the last person with a balloon or balloons. The game can be played with or without boundaries.

Variations: (1) Play the game with teams rather than individually. In this version, at the end of the game, the team with one or more players with a balloon is the winner. (2) Tie the balloons in different places (around waist, on wrists, etc.) and allow hands for bursting other players' balloons.

HACKY SACK

Grades: K–6

Purposes: To improve eye/foot coordination and flexibility
To provide aerobic exercise
To provide practice of lead-up skills for soccer

Equipment: A Hacky Sack for each group. If Hacky Sacks are not available, a substitute foot bag may be used (bean bag, wad of newspaper or scrap paper, etc.)

Description: Divide the players into groups of three to six. Each group is given a Hacky Sack or similar object to kick, finds a small space, and forms a tight circle. The object of the game is for the group to keep the Hacky Sack aloft for as long as possible. A rally is started when the player holding the Hacky Sack throws it gently to another player in the group. Any part of the body may be used to keep the Hacky Sack in play except hands and arms. Using feet, knees, chest, and head shots the players pass the Hacky Sack around the circle randomly, trying to keep it aloft for several kicks in a row.

Variations: (1) For younger students and beginning players, a small balloon may be used to allow more reaction time before each kick. (2) For competitive Hacky Sack, have groups count the number of consecutive kicks each rally and see which group gets the highest number without letting the Hacky Sack touch the ground. (3) Establish a rotation system whereby players are constantly playing with new teammates. (4) Turn on a record or tape and play "Musical Hacky Sack."

SWING THE SACK

Grades: 2–6

Purposes: To promote physical fitness
To improve coordination and agility

Equipment: One piece of rope tied to a stuffed bag

Description: Move desks aside. Have players stand in a circle, arm's length apart. The sack-swinger stands in the center and swings the sack at ankle height. The swinger holds the rope so that everybody must jump to keep from having their feet hit. Whoever the sack touches becomes the new swinger.

Variations: (1) Require players to hop on one foot while trying to avoid the sack. (2) Have players form groups of two. One player must close his eyes and jump on the command of his partner (they may hold hands).

ANKLE HOP

Grades: 2–6

Purposes: To improve overall physical fitness
To enhance coordination and agility
To develop arts and crafts skills

Equipment: Each child will need: a plastic margarine container and two lids, or an old tennis ball
Approximately four feet of rope, twine, or string
Some masking tape

Description: This is a combination craft project/indoor recess activity. After making the Ankle Hop equipment, the children can enjoy jumping over them each time they make a complete revolution.

Construction:

1. Place a small hole in the side of the margarine container.
2. Insert one end of the rope and knot it in order to prevent it from slipping out of the container.
3. Tape the lid shut.
4. Cut the center out of the second lid leaving a border of about one inch. Tape the inside of the ring to prevent scratching of the ankle.
5. Secure the other end of the rope to the plastic circle.
6. Same procedures may be followed using an old tennis ball rather than the margarine containers.

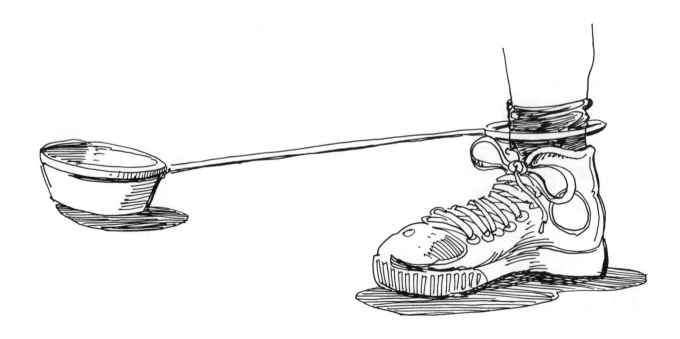

ALL-IN SIMON SAYS

Grades: 2–6

Purposes: To develop listening and communication skills
To increase flexibility
To promote cooperation

Equipment: None

Description: Break the group into two, three, or four equal groups. A leader is chosen for each group. At the same time, each leader says, "Simon says," and performs various movements, and the other players are to imitate the movements. If a leader neglects to say, "Simon says," before performing a movement and a player imitates the movement, she is transferred to one of the other games. A pattern of rotation should be established. In this version of Simon Says, *no one is eliminated* from the action.

Variations: (1) End the game with a standard round of Simon Says with the whole group included. (2) Have students perform a task before entering the next group after being eliminated from another group (push-ups, jumps over a chair, math problems, etc.).

CLEAN UP YOUR ROOM

Grades: 2–6

Purposes: To improve physical fitness
To increase flexibility
To have fun

Equipment: Several balls, socks, wads of paper
and/or any handy objects

Description: Push desks aside. Have the group form two equal teams. Mark a center line of the play area with chalk, tape, or string. Each team scatters on half of the play area, sitting on the floor. All available objects are scattered around the floor. At the signal (whistle, music, etc.), players on both sides throw as many objects as possible into the opposing team's half of the play area. Players continue to throw objects back and forth as fast as they can until the signal to stop is given. The winning team is the one with the cleanest room (fewest objects on its side of the room) when the signal to stop is given. Have players divide the objects equally again, and play another round. Play several rounds and keep score of total wins!

Variations: Play "Task Clean Up Your Room" in which the winning team for each round decides upon a task for the opposing team's members to accomplish (sit-ups, push-ups, math problem, etc.).

KNEE AND FLEE

Grades: 2–6

Purposes: To improve coordination, flexibility and agility
To improve throwing skills
To have fun

Equipment: Several foam rubber balls, balled-up socks, and/or wads of paper

Description: Have the players scatter themselves about the play area. The foam balls, etc., are scattered around the floor. At the signal (whistle, music, etc.), players pick up one ball at a time and try to hit as many people as possible in the knees with the ball in a given time period while they are dodging the balls thrown by others. Change the game frequently by calling different body parts to be hit (Toe and Go, Bun and Run, Burn 'em in the Sternum, Back Attack, etc.).

Variations: (1) Have players throw with non-dominant hand only. (2) Play an elimination round in which players who have been hit sit at the edge of the play area, and see who can be the last one hit.

NEW WAVE ERASER TAG

Grades: 2–6

Purposes: To improve quickness and agility
To improve balance

Equipment: An eraser or similar object which can be balanced on the head

Description: Players scatter about the play area. One person is chosen to be *It* and he/she must balance an eraser on his/her head while attempting to tag another player. Players use quickness and agility to avoid being tagged by It. If It drops the eraser in an attempt to tag someone, he must replace it and begin chasing again. When It successfully tags another player, the two switch places and the game continues.

Variations: (1) Have two or three Its at the same time to add excitement to the game. (2) Play traditional Eraser Tag, in which two teams are formed and It chases a player from the other team one-on-one until he either tags the opponent or drops the eraser, and points are scored accordingly.

JUG TAG

Grades: 2–6

Purposes: To improve quickness and agility
To provide exercise for overall physical fitness

Equipment: One plastic jug with the bottom cut off
A foam rubber ball or wad of paper

Description: Players scatter about the play area. One person is chosen to be *It,* and is given the jug and foam rubber ball. Players try to avoid being hit by the ball as It attempts to fling the ball out of the jug and hit someone below the shoulders. When It hits someone, the two trade places and the game continues.

Variations: (1) Play "Spot Jug Tag" in which It must hit someone in a predetermined spot (foot, rear, etc.). (2) Use two or three jugs and have several Its at the same time.

BOP TAG

Grades: 2–6

Purposes: To improve overall physical fitness
To improve agility

Equipment: A foam rubber bat, sock stuffed with rags, or a small pillow to use as a "bopper"

Description: Have players spread out over the entire play area. One person is chosen to be *It* and is given the bopper. On the signal to begin, everyone tries to avoid being tagged with the bopper. When It successfully bops someone, the person who was hit becomes the new chaser, and the game continues. Hits above the shoulders do not count.

FOAM FILLED BOPPER

Variations: (1) Play "Spot Bop Tag" in which the leader assigns particular spots to be bopped (knees, toes, elbows, etc.). (2) Use two or three boppers and have more than one It in the game.

SOCK THE BOX

Grades: 4–6

Purposes: To promote cooperation
To develop baseball lead-up skills (throwing for accuracy)
To improve coordination and fitness

Equipment: One to three boxes
As many sponge rubber balls as possible
(If no sponge rubber balls are available, have each student "ball-up" one of his/her socks to throw)

Description: Push desks aside. Divide class into two equal teams. Teams line up on opposite sides of the room. Place one or more boxes an equal distance from each team. When the signal is given, both teams begin firing at the boxes, trying to move them across their opponent's point line (tape or chalk line). One point is scored each time a team is successful. The game can end on time limit or point limit. It is helpful to assign one player from each team as shagger for balls or socks left in the middle.

Variations: (1) Have players throw with non-dominant arm. (2) To add excitement, use one or two large Nerf Balls (soccer ball size) together with the rest of the objects to be thrown.

BLAST BALL

Grades: 4–6

Purposes: To encourage teamwork
                To increase flexibility, strength, and coordination

Equipment: Foam rubber balls
                 Tape or butcher paper

Description: Push the desks aside. The players sit on the floor with their feet out in front of them. They must remain in this position. They can slide to a different location on the floor when they do not have the ball. The game is started with a center drop between two players. Each team tries to score a goal by passing the ball to one of its players who is in position to throw the ball into the goal. The goal should be about four feet high and three feet wide and can be designated on the wall on each end of the room with tape or a piece of butcher paper. A neutral zone should be designed in front of each goal to keep the emphasis on offensive play.

Variation: Make all players throw with non-dominant arm.

Suggestion: Have one team tie a sock, scarf, piece of material, or strip of paper around one arm to aid in identifying teammates.

GERM WARS

Grades: 4–6

Purposes: To promote cooperation
To increase physical fitness
To develop throwing skills

Equipment: Several foam rubber balls or balled-up socks
Two plastic bats (or padded yardsticks)

Description: Push desks aside. Divide the room into two equal halves with a piece of tape or string, or make a chalk line. Have the players form two teams and face each other on opposite sides of the room. The teams are armed with lethal "germs" (foam balls). The players attempt to "infect" the opposition by hitting them with germs to immobilize them. If a player is hit with a germ, he falls dramatically to the ground and is frozen. Each team has a doctor with a syringe (plastic bat or padded yardstick), who can give a shot to a frozen player and revive him. The goal is to infect the opposing doctor, because he cannot give himself a shot and no one else can become the doctor. If the doctor is hit, the game is over.

Variations: (1) Continue playing after the doctor is hit until all of the opposition is eliminated. (2) Have players throw with non-dominant hand only.

FLAG TAG

Grades: 4–6

Purposes: To improve overall physical fitness
To promote group cooperation
To increase coordination and agility

Equipment: A flag for each player, (a strip of material, an old sock, football flag, or strip of construction paper)

Description: Push desks aside. Each player is given a flag. One player is chosen to be *It* and gives up his flag. The object is for It to procure the flags of other players. When It captures a flag, the one captured also becomes an It and attempts to get flags. Soon, more and more players have become Its, and the flag people are dwindling rapidly. The last person to be captured starts off as It for the next round. Flags should be tucked into waistband or in pocket.

Variations: (1) Play a few rounds of "No Rules Flag Tag" in which players are allowed to protect their flag in any possible manner that is safe (hold on to it, back up against the wall, lay down with flag under body, etc.). (2) Have players use a method of locomotion other than running (hopping, crab walking, etc.).

DRIBBLE TAG

Grades: 4–6

Purposes: To provide lead-up skills for basketball
To improve overall fitness

Equipment: One or two basketballs, rubber balls, or soccer balls.

Description: Push the desks aside to allow as much space in the room as possible. One player is chosen to be *It*. The rest of the players scatter about the play area. The object is for It to get close enough to another player to tag him/her, while dribbling a basketball. When It successfully tags another player while controlling the basketball with a dribble, the two exchange positions, and the game continues.

Variations: (1) Play with two or three Its and use additional basketballs. (2) Change the task for It (run with a ball between the knees, dribble with non-dominant hand, balance a Frisbee on head, etc.).

CRAB KICK

Grades: 4–6

Purposes: To increase strength and endurance
                        To provide practice of lead-up games for soccer

Equipment: A ball of any type

Description: Push the desks aside. Divide the group into two equal teams and have them sit down at opposite ends of the room. Place a desk at each end of the room to serve as a goal. Place the ball in the center of the room. On the signal to begin, players crab walk to the ball and proceed to kick it toward their goal and score. Players must stay in the crab walk position the entire game or be penalized with a free kick for the opposing team. For other infractions, normal soccer rules apply. There are no out-of-bounds areas, thus the action continues until one team scores a goal. After a goal is scored, the ball is placed in the center of the room, and the game continues.

Variations: (1) Have players scoot about in their chairs for a round instead of crab walking. (2) Put two or three balls in play at the same time.

SCOOT HOOP

Grades: 4–6

Purposes: To increase strength and endurance
To practice lead-up skills for basketball

Equipment: A ball of any type

Description: Push desks aside. Divide the group into two even teams and have players sit in their chairs at opposite ends of the room. Place a waste basket on the floor or on top of desks at each end of the room, and place a ball in the center of the room. On the signal to begin, both teams scoot in their chairs to get the ball, and proceed to move the ball toward their basket and attempt to score. The ball need not be dribbled; instead, players may balance it on their lap while scooting or use passes to advance the ball. All players must stay on their chair or a foul is called. When a player is fouled, or someone scoots illegally, foul shots are taken as in basketball. For other infractions, normal basketball rules apply. The team with the most points at the end of the time period wins.

Variations: (1) Play with two or three balls at the same time. (2) Play "Crab Walk Hoop," in which partners move about on all fours, belly up, rather than scooting in their chairs.

CLASSROOM TRIATHLON

Grades: 4–6

Purposes: To increase endurance
To improve overall physical fitness
To promote fair play and cooperation

Equipment: None

Description: Designate three starting areas as follows:
1) The track starting line
2) The Air Bike* area
3) The rowboat area

Divide the players into three groups, and assign each group to one of the three starting areas. Establish a pattern of rotation to be followed by participants as they work their way through the events. On the signal to begin, each participant attempts to successfully complete all three events without stopping. The events can be set up as follows:

1) The 20-mile run (walk fast around the room 20 times)
2) The 200-mile bike race (200 leg kicks, Air Bike* style)
3) The 300-mile row (300 pretend boat rows)

The first person to successfully complete all three events is declared the winner. Players who finish early may become fans and enthusiastically encourage those still participating.

Variations: (1) Change the events and have another triathlon (rope jumping, push-ups, running in place, etc.). (2) Play the game in pairs ("tag-team" style). In this version, tired players may tag a teammate when they are tired, and the other half of the team takes over for awhile.

*See the Air Bike instructions in Section VII.

V
Academic
Action

PASS AND COUNT

Grades: K–2

Purposes: To reinforce number identification and counting skills
To improve hand/eye coordination

Equipment: One ball of any type

Description: Players may sit or stand in a circle, or they may remain at their desks. The object of the game is to pass the ball from player to player without letting it drop and stopping it at a designated number. The leader calls out any number. The players pass the ball around the room, counting passes aloud. When the designated number is reached, the child holding the ball raises it overhead and becomes the new leader. He calls a new number and the game continues. If the ball is dropped, the counting must begin again, starting with the next player.

Variations: (1) Have players count by 2s, 5s, or 10s. (2) Have players throw with non-dominant hand, or catch one-handed.

ALPHABET RELAY

Grades: K–6

Purposes: To reinforce knowledge of letter and number recognition
To improve flexibility

Equipment: None

Description: Provide adequate space in front of the room or push desks aside. Have students form groups of 10 to 16, and then have the groups scatter themselves around the play area. The leader should be elevated in order to better detect the winner. The leader calls a letter, such as the letter *T,* and all groups quickly form that letter. The group forming the correct letter first scores a point for their team.

Variations: (1) Use numbers instead of letters. (2) For younger students, have them form letters by contorting their own bodies to represent letters or numbers.

BLACKBOARD RELAYS

Grades: K–6

Purposes: To reinforce mathematics and language skills
To provide movement and exercise

Equipment: Several pieces of chalk

Description: Divide the class into equal groups of 4 to 8 players. Each team occupies a row of seats. Chalk can be placed on the first desk or it can be left in the tray of the blackboard. On a signal, the first player in each row walks quickly to the blackboard, makes the appropriate mark on the board with the chalk, returns to his seat and hands the chalk to the person sitting behind him in the row. Each team member follows the same procedure. The winning team is the one which has the last player in the row return to his seat first.

Variations: (1) Each person writes a designated number on the board. (2) Team members write a designated number on the board until the last person in the row; he must write the sum. Each person writes a word on the board. The object is to have a completed sentence after the last player has finished.(4) For older students, include multiplication and division in the relays.

MATH SCRAMBLE*

Grades: K–6

Purposes: To provide for the review or reinforcement of most mathematical concepts
To provide mild exercise

Equipment: A set of ten number cards (one number per card, from 0 through 9) for each team (For best results, make each set from cards of a different color.)

Description: Have players form groups of ten and give each player a number card (all players with numbers on red cards are on the same team, all green are a team, etc.). Capable players can be given two number cards, or assigned jobs such as judge or scorekeeper, if the number of students won't allow for even teams of ten. To play "Scramble" the leader calls out a math problem of any kind, and each student quickly solves the problem mentally, or with pencil and paper, and checks to see if his number card is part of the answer. Players having numbers that are in the answer walk rapidly to the front of the room and display their cards in proper order, as viewed by the leader. A point is then scored by each team showing the correct answer, and a bonus point is also awarded to the team that was both first and correct.

Variations: (1) Use number puzzles or long sequences and see which team can concentrate through really tough problems. (2) Utilize the versatility of the game by giving problems in decimals, fractions, Roman numerals, word problems, etc. Certain students can also be given decimal point cards, and others remainder cards for division.

---

*Overholt, James L., *Dr. Jim's Elementary Math Prescriptions: Activities/Aids/Games to Help Children Learn Elementary Mathematics.* (Glenview, Illinois: Scott, Foresman and Co., Goodyear Division, 1978) p. 115.

MATH BALL*

Grades: K–6

Purposes: To provide for the reinforcement and review of counting, mental addition, subtraction, multiplication, and division (Decimal and fraction understandings can also be reviewed with this activity.)

To improve hand/eye coordination

Equipment: A tennis ball, softball, or small playground ball

Description: Divide a ball into several sections with a felt-tip marker. Write a number in each section as shown in the diagram. Students may sit in their desks, or sit or stand in a circle. The leader calls out a mathematical function (addition, subtraction, multiplication, or division) and the player with the ball throws it to someone else. The player who catches the ball identifies the numbers under his thumb and middle finger, and performs the appropriate computations orally. He then tosses the ball to someone else and the game continues.

Variations: (1) Play an elimination round in which players remain in the game only if they give correct answers. (2) To increase the difficulty level, use three or more fingers and/or two or more operations. (3) Play a round where trick shots may be used (bounce passes, behind the back, etc.). (4) Primary students might bounce the answers and have their peers count the bounces as a check.

*Overholt, James. L., *Dr. Jim's Elementary Math Prescriptions: Activities/Aids/Games to Help Children Learn Elementary Mathematics.* (Glenview, Illinois: Scott, Foresman and Co., Goodyear Division, 1978) p. 11.

PEOPLE-TO-PEOPLE

Grades: K–6

Purposes: To increase flexibility

To enjoy the activity

To reinforce the learning of body parts for younger students, and the identification of bones for older students

Equipment: None

Description: This game can be played without rearranging the classroom, or the desks may be pushed aside. Divide the group into partners. Have everyone stand in a circle next to their partner. The leader stands in the center of the circle. He sets a beat by clapping or snapping his fingers and chanting "people-to-people" while encouraging everyone to join in the chant. After repeating the chant a few times, the leader substitutes the name of a body part for each word ("people-to-people") in the chant while keeping the same rhythm. As the players repeat the chant, they assume the position the chant suggested with their partner. For example, if "shoulder-to-ankle" was called, one player would touch his shoulder to his partner's ankle. Players continue to match body parts according to the leader's instructions until the leader calls "people-to-people." This is the signal for everyone to scamper around and find a new partner, including the leader. Players return to the circle with their new partner, except for the person who is left out. This person becomes the new leader and starts up the chant.

Variations: (1) Instead of pairing up, have students form groups of three or four each round. (2) For older students, who may be studying the human body, call out bones instead of body parts (femur-to-femur).

LISTEN UP

Grades: K–6

Purposes: To encourage careful listening
To have a great time

Equipment: Any story or poem that is interesting to the students, and at their reading level.
Directions that tell the students what physical activity or sound effect they are to enact for designated words in the reading selection

Description: The story or poem is read aloud by the teacher. Each time the students hear a designated word, they must do the physical activity or sound effect that is associated with it. For the following "Indians and Cowboys" story, these sounds and motions will be used:

Word	Motion of Sound
Indians	Say Woo—Woo and do an Indian type dance.
cowboys	Walk bow-legged.
time	Say Tick-Tock and swing arms as a pendulum.
peace	Get into a sleeping position.
stream	Move hand in wave motion and say Ripple-Ripple.
lake	Make a swimming motion.
broken	Make any breaking motion.
cows	Say Moo-Moo and move on hands and feet.
guns	Say Bang-Bang.
arrows	Say Whiz-Whiz.
listened	Put hand to ear.

A Story:

The Indians and Cowboys

Once upon a (*time*) there lived in a big valley some (*Indians*) and some (*cowboys*). The (*Indians*) lived by the (*stream*) and the (cowboys) had a ranch house near a (*lake*). They had lived in (*peace*) for a long (*time*), but one day the (*peace*) was (*broken*). Some (*cows*) were missing, and the (*cowboys*) said that the (*Indians*) had taken them. They all became angry and soon were shooting at each other. The (*cowboys*) fired their (*guns*) and the (*Indians*) shot with their bows and (*arrows*). (*Guns*) fired rapidly and (*arrows*) flew through the air from morning until afternoon. Then a different sound was heard. Everyone stopped shooting and (*listened*). Then they heard it again! It went moo. It sounded like a (*cow*)? The (*cowboys*) raised a white flag, and so did the (*Indians*). They went into the forest to check, and do you know what they found? You guessed it, they found not one (*cow*), but a whole herd. The (*cowboys*) put their (*guns*) away and the (*Indians*) put their (*arrows*) in their quivers. That was the last (*time*) they had any trouble and they lived in (*peace*) for years and years.

BULL'S-EYE SPELLING

Grades: K–6

Purposes: To improve spelling (or number) skills
To improve hand/eye coordination and throwing skills

Equipment: One or more foam rubber balls or wads of paper or rags

Description: Draw the letters of the alphabet on the chalkboard and put a large circle around each letter. Divide the group into two equal teams and have teams form lines at the back of the room. The leader gives the first team a word to spell. The first player steps up to a designated throwing line and throws the ball at the first letter in the word. Each player gets one throw per turn. The object is for the team to hit the correct letters in the fewest number of throws possible. The second team is given a word with the same number of letters, and the process is repeated. A point can be scored for each round won, or the game can be played just for fun.

Variations: (1) Play the game using math by writing the numbers 0 through 9 on the board and have teams solve a problem, then hit the correct numbers for the answer. (2) Have players form smaller groups and have two or three games going at different chalkboards. (3) For young students, simplify the task to identifying and hitting one letter or number.

YARN SHAPES

Grades: K–6

Purposes: To introduce or reinforce geometric shapes
To function as a cooperative group
To actively participate in a math task

Equipment: Six or seven pieces of yarn, string or rope that are each 20 to 30 feet long (Tie the ends of each piece together to form large loops.)

Description: Designate four to six students to work with each loop. Place them at evenly spaced intervals around the loop and have them hold it waist high. Then denote a geometric figure that they are to form with the yarn; simple figures might include triangles, rectangles and squares. Slightly more difficult shapes to form will be pentagons, rhombuses, scalene triangles, circles and ovals (the yarn may be placed on the floor in order to show curves). Three-dimensional figures will provide a challenge for the most advanced students; they might create frameworks for rectangular solids or cubes and triangular or square-based pyramids.

SISTINE ART

Grades: K–6

Purposes: To stimulate an appreciation of Michelangelo's painting
To provide exercise for the large muscles of the arm
To enhance fine motor skills

Equipment: Art paper
Masking tape
A variety of colored pencils, crayons, marking pens and/or brushes and "thick" paint

Description: You might begin with a description and discussion of how Michelangelo spent four years lying on his back in order to paint the frescoes decorating the ceiling of the Sistine Chapel (pictures of this painting can also be found in most encyclopedias and in many art appreciation books). Next, each student should design or select a scene that he or she will create in much the same manner as Michelangelo did. Then have everyone tape a large sheet of art paper to the underside of his or her desk. Finally, while lying on his or her back, each student is to use the available art supplies to create a Sistine-type art painting.

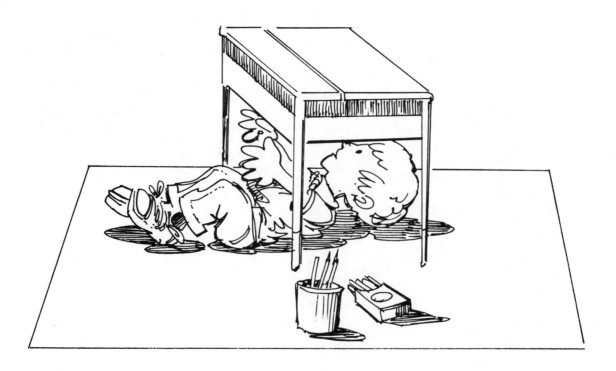

GUESS WHO

Grades: K–6

Purposes: To improve listening skills
To have fun

Equipment: None

Description: Have players stand in a group with eyes closed and backs to the center of the room. The leader taps one person on the shoulder, and that person moves to the center of the room. The person who was chosen begins by saying one word in a disguised voice. The other players raise their hands to be called on to make a guess as to who the mystery voice belongs to. If they don't succeed in three to five tries, the mystery person says a sentence in a disguised voice. The person who guesses the mystery person's name correctly gets to tap the next mystery person on the shoulder.

Variations: (1) Have players read a passage from a book in their disguised voice. (2) Have players laugh in a disguised way instead of speaking.

ANSWER ACTIONS

Grades: K–6

Purposes: To help students learn how to frame questions
To provide non-verbal answers
To enjoy mild exercise

Equipment: None required (but some students may want to use paper and pencil to write their questions)

Description: Have each student, or cooperative teams of students, phrase questions that can be answered with some action(s). For a simple question such as how much is 3 + 4, the result might be indicated by hopping 7 times. A slightly harder question like how do you spell academic, could be answered with finger spelling. A more complex question such as what sequence of events provide the tuna that you eat in a tunafish sandwich, might be acted out by several students portraying catching tuna in the ocean, cleaning, cooking, canning, shipping, marketing, preparing the tuna at home, etc.

Variations: During subsequent sessions, require that questions be asked at increasingly more difficult levels involving knowledge, comprehension, application, analysis, synthesis, and possibly evaluation.

RUN AROUND 'RITHMETIC

Grades: 2–6

Purposes: To provide for the reinforcement and review of addition, subtraction, multiplication, and division skills (Decimals and fractions can also be incorporated.)

To provide exercise

Equipment: None

Description: Have the group form two equal teams. Teams form separate circles, either sitting or standing. Each player is given a number. When the leader calls a number, each player having that number tries to be the first player back to his original place first after running around his circle. A point is scored for the team whose player gets back first. Addition, subtraction, multiplication, and division may be used: for example, a 2 and 4 might be called for addition, in which case the number six player for each team would run.

Variations: (1) Have each row be a team and the runner circle his row and get back to his seat. (2) Change the method of locomotion (skip, hop, walk backwards, etc.).

TEAM SPELLING

Grades: 2–6

Purposes: To introduce and review spelling words
To enhance overall physical fitness

Equipment: A set of alphabet cards for each group

Description: Have players form groups of five to ten. Place a complete set of alphabet cards near each group. The leader pronounces a short word, and the first few players in each group—as many as there are letters in the word—hurry to the cards, select the proper cards, then go to the front of the room and arrange themselves in the proper order. The team finishing the word first scores a point. Words must be selected carefully to avoid duplication of letters. Players may indicate double letters by holding a fist next to their letter. If a letter is used twice, the player may keep moving back and forth, or hold a fist next to her letter. Have players rotate so that each person gets an equal number of turns.

Variations: (1) For younger students, call only a single letter. Then have individual players select that same letter and go to the front of the room with it. (2) Play "task" team spelling, in which players must perform a predetermined task before selecting their letters (such as dribble a ball five times, jump as high as they can ten times, etc.).

BEAN BAG MATH

Grades: 2–6

Purposes: To provide for the reinforcement and review of addition, subtraction, multiplication, and division skills

To improve hand/eye coordination

Equipment: Two bean bags for each row of players

Description: At the front of each row, construct a nine-square diagram with each square about 12 inches wide (this can be done with chalk, or drawn on construction paper and kept for future use; students can draw their own diagrams to lessen work for leader). The squares are randomly numbered 1 through 9. For more advanced students, larger numbers may be substituted to reinforce multipication and division facts. Each player tosses two bean bags toward the target, one at a time. Players add, subtract, multiply, or divide the two numbers indicated by the position of the bean bags. The leader or selected students may act as judges for correct and incorrect answers. A point is scored for each correct answer. The game can be played for an individual winner, or the winner may be the row with the highest score at the end of the given time period.

Variations: (1) Scramble player position each round to provide interaction between different people. (2) Have players use trick shots (spin around and throw, behind the back, etc.).

HOPSCOTCH MATH

Grades: 2–6

Purposes: To provide for the reinforcement and review of addition, subtraction, multiplication, and division skills (Decimals and fractions can also be used with this activity.)

To improve leg strength and agility

Equipment: A few sections of butcher paper

Description: The leader may make the grids by drawing 16 one-foot squares and labeling them as shown in the diagram below. An alternative is to have the players mark their own grids on the floor with chalk. Have the players take their shoes off to save the grids. Each row is a team. One player goes up to the grid and hops on one square (a number), then to another square (a plus, minus, multiplication, or division sign), then to another square (a number), then to another square (the equal sign), then the last square he hops to will be the answer. Selected players may be chosen to be judges for each row. Players may choose their own problems to be solved, but they cannot repeat problems solved by other players. Teams keep their own scores, or judges may keep score on the board. The team with the most points at the end of a given time period is the winner.

Variations: (1) As a math review, the leader may call out the problems to be solved, in which case each player hops through the same problem on a given round. (2) Play a round where neighboring rows compete against each other. In this version, the two participants give each other problems to solve. (3) For older students, allow them to make problems using two or three numbers.

SHOW THIS MATH

Grades: 2–6

Purposes: To correlate mental mathematics and physical activity
To enjoy both the mathematics and the exercise

Equipment: None

Description: The teacher, or a student, leads the entire class in this activity by calling out a mathematics problem which each student must solve mentally. After a few moments the leader names the physical activity to be done and says, "Ready, begin." The students must then repeat the designated physical activity the number of times required to answer the mathematics problem. For example, the leader might say, "The problem is $9 + 5$ and the activitiy is jumping jacks." The leader signals when to begin, and the students do 14 jumping jacks in unison. When finished, the leader should say, "$9 + 5$ was correctly answered with 14 jumping jacks."

Variations: (1) The difficulty level of the mathematics problems needs to match student capabilities. (2) When difficult problems are assigned, pencil and paper computations may be allowed.

BALANCE-IT BOX ACTIVITIES

Grades: 2–6

Purposes: To provide vocabulary reinforcement and physical activity
To enhance small and large motor skills
To enjoy the activity

Equipment: A small cardboard box and a pencil and paper for each student.
Two boxes (for the teacher)

Description: Each student writes a vocabulary word, a number (not more than 20) and a physical activity on her (or his) paper. She places the paper in her box and goes to the front of the room where she attempts to balance it on boxes that are already in place. The teacher had started the process by placing two penalty boxes on the floor. The balancing continues until all of the students have balanced their boxes. If a student should knock down some or all of the balanced boxes, he receives a penalty and must do whatever the teacher has written and placed in the penalty boxes (the students know that one message will give a free turn, but the other will require rigorous exercise). When all of the boxes have been successfully balanced, the teacher commands, "Blow them down." The students then blow until the boxes begin to fall. Then each student grabs a box, other than her own, and opens it to see what word she must tell the meaning of, and the physical activity she must do. When all students have completed their tasks, the boxes may be restacked for another try or put away.

PANTOMIME A VERB

Grades: 2–6

Purposes: To reinforce language and vocabulary understandings
To correlate physical activity and language arts

Equipment: A container full of slips of paper with an action verb written on each (The set of action verbs might include such words as run, swim, drink, sat, etc.)

Description: This pantomime activity may be enacted with the whole class or in small groups. The teacher or leader has each student secretly draw an action verb from the container. At her turn, the student pantomimes the activity associated with her word. The other students take turns trying to guess the verb, but when doing so, they must use the verb they are guessing in a complete sentence. When someone identifies the verb, that person moves to the front of the group and pantomimes another action verb. The process continues until all of the verbs have been identified.

Variations: (1) Young children may need help reading their verb and/or coaching to know how to portray it. (2) Older students might try to pantomime verbs that are by nature more abstract (such as leak, fortify, irk, etc.).

PEOPLE SUBSETS

Grades: 2–6

Purposes: To reinforce student understandings of mathematical subsets in real life
To provide physical activity

Equipment: None

Description: The leader might ask all of the people with blond hair to stand and each do three toe-touches. After doing so, it should be noted that these people are a real-life mathematical subset of all of the students in the class. Next, all people wearing blue socks might stand and each do six knee-bends. Point out that this is another real-life subset, and that a few people belonged to both subsets. As soon as the students fully understand the process, let them take turns designating different subsets and the physical activities that their named subsets are to do.

Variations: (1) Have two or three subsets identified and see how many people are in the intersection. (2) Call on selected people to stand and have the other students attempt to name the attribute(s) of the "new" subset.

ACTIVE ANSWERS

Grades: 2–6

Purposes: To reinforce mathematical concepts
To relate math results to physical activities

Equipment: None

Description: In this activity the answers to mathematical computations are to be shown in an active manner. For example, if the problem is $5 + 7 = \underline{\quad}$, the answer might be indicated by having 5 children count off as they each do a pushup, and then 7 more children continue the count as each does his or her pushup, until a total of 12 is indicated. More complex mathematical computations can also be completed in a similar manner. With the problem $7 \times 6 = \underline{\quad}$, the result might be shown by having 7 students take turns doing 6 jumping jacks each, with the count accumulating from one student to the next, until 42 is attained.

READ, WRITE AND RUN

Grades: 2–6

Purposes: To correlate reading, record keeping, and exercise

Equipment: Each team needs—
A record keeping form
a pencil
a stopwatch or other timing device
someone to operate the watch

Description: Each team will be doing the same activities, but they are scrambled (see the samples below) so that the participants will be doing their exercises at different times. At the "go" signal, the first member of each team runs to the exercise area, notes activity #1, and does as many of that particular exercise as she can in one minute. She is then allowed another 30 seconds to record her number of exercises and run back to her team. At exactly one and one-half minutes, the "go" signal is given again, and the procedure is repeated. This continues until all team members have had their turns. The winning team is the one which accumulates the greatest total number for all of the exercises.

Team A	Team B	Team C
_11_ push-ups	_17_ sit-ups	_14_ jumping jacks
_12_ jumping jacks	____ knee bends	_26_ shoulder rolls
____ knee bends	____ push-ups	____ sit-ups
____ shoulder rolls	____ jumping jacks	____ push-ups

Variation: The record keeping forms for very young students might have the activities pictured, rather than written.

WORD ART

Grades: 2–6

Purposes: To stimulate creativity and artistic expression
To provide exercise

Equipment: None

Description: Divide the group into two equal teams. One representative from each team goes up to the leader, who gives them a word quietly so that the rest of the group cannot hear. The representatives hurry to the board and draw pictures to represent the word. A person giving the correct identification first scores a point for his team. The winning team is the one with the most points after a given time period.

Variations: (1) Play "Task Word Art" in which representatives must complete a task on their way to the board (hop around one row of desks, dribble a ball 10 times, etc.). (2) Divide the group into smaller teams to allow more participation.

GRAPHATHON

Grades: 2–6

Purposes: To provide interesting and meaningful data to be used in graphing assignments
To provide a set of activities which will help to develop an unlimited number of physical education skills

Equipment: Objects necessary for participation in center activities

Description: This activity helps motivate children and stimulate interest in learning to read and make graphs. Students participate in several center activities, and collect data about themselves for their graphs. Center activities might include: number of times players can jump rope in one minute (or without missing); number of inches players can jump from a standing start; number of successful attempts out of ten throwing a wad of paper into a trash can; amount of time players can hop on one foot without stopping; javelin throw—where players record the number of inches they can throw a straw; shot put—where students record the number of inches they can shot put a cotton ball; and any other activity that lends itself to the collection of data.

Have the players pair off. Each pair completes each activity, and each player records all of his results along the way. These scores are raw data to be used for a myriad of future graphing activities.

Variations: Use mental activities as well as physical activities (how many words can a player make using the letters in the name of the school, number of math problems solved correctly out of ten, etc.).

PLUNGER MAN

Grades: 2–6

Purposes: To reinforce number identification, addition, and multiplication skills
To facilitate quick reflexes

Equipment: A pair of dice and a toilet plunger (for each group of 3-8 players)
A rubber washer tied to a piece of string approximately three feet long (for each player)

Description: The game can be played in groups of three to eight players. Participants sit on the floor, forming a circle. One player is chosen to be the Plunger Man. He holds both the plunger and the pair of dice. The other players put their washers into the center of the circle and prepare to quickly yank them away. The Plunger Man rolls the dice toward the center of the circle. When a sum of 7 or 11 occurs, all players must yank their washers out of the circle before the Plunger Man can pin them down. Any player caught by the Plunger Man is out of the game for that round. When only one player remains, he becomes the new Plunger Man. (The Plunger Man may attempt to fake players on a sum other than 7 or 11 by flinching, but he may not lift the plunger off the ground to fake. If the Plunger Man lifts the plunger off the ground by mistake or during a fake attempt, all players are back in the game for that round. If a player yanks his washer by mistake or during a legal fake, he is eliminated from that round.)

Variations: (1) Change the sums on which players are to yank the washers. (2) Have players multiply rather than add, establish alternate products on which they are to yank the washers. (3) For younger students, simply have players use one die and yank the washers when a predetermined number occurs.

SPELLING WITH A TWIST

Grades: 2–6

Purposes: To review spelling words
To provide exercise for overall physical fitness

Equipment: None

Description: Have players line up in two equal teams. Give out words for spelling which include as many vowels as possible. The two players in front of the lines walk, hop, skip, or run to the front of the room. Each player is given a word to spell. Players score one point for their team each time a word is spelled correctly. When spelling the words, players pronounce all of the letters in the word except the vowels. For the vowels, the following are required:

> A = Five push-ups
> E = Run in place ten steps
> I = Point to own eye
> O = Point to own mouth
> U = Point at the leader

The team with the most points at the end of a given time period wins!

Variations: (1) Change the requirements for vowels. (2) Change the task for players making their way to the front of the room.

THE DIRECTION CONNECTION*

Grades: 2–6

Purposes: To introduce, reinforce, or review the concept of compass directions
To provide for exercise and physical fitness

Equipment: Signs with the four major compass points printed on them

Description: Print the four major directions (north, south, east, west) on large pieces of paper and tape them on the appropriate walls of the room. Divide the group into two equal teams. The leader calls out one of the directions, and both teams must stand up and face the appropriately labeled wall. A point is scored for the first team to have all members facing in the proper direction. The winning team is the first to reach a given number of points.

Variations: (1) Divide the players into four groups and play "Musical Directions" in which players walk around the room until a signal is given, then players scramble for a position. The leader calls one of the directions, and those players are eliminated from the game, and so on. (2) For more advanced students, include northeast, northwest, southeast, and southwest.

---

*Cotler, Harold L., *Galaxy of Games, Stunts, and Activities for Elementary Physical Education*, West Nyack, NY: Parker Publishing Company, Inc., 1980.

ARITHMETIC SPIN THE PLATE

Grades: 2–6

Purposes: To provide for the reinforcement or review of addition, subtraction, multiplication, and division skills (Decimals and fractions might also be used in this game.)
To enhance physical fitness

Equipment: A plastic plate, pie pan, lid, or anything that will spin

Description: Push desks aside. The players form a circle, and number off consecutively with numbers above ten. One player is chosen to go to the center of the circle. He spins the plate and identifies the one who is to catch it by calling an arithmetic problem to indicate the player's number. For example, player 10 might be indicated as number 2×5 or number $20 - 10$. Addition, subtraction, multiplication, or division may be used. If the player catches the plate before it falls, he becomes the next center player. If the plate stops before the identified player can catch it, the original center player may spin the plate again.

Variations: (1) Use a balloon instead of a plate, in which case the player must catch it before it hits the ground. (2) For younger students, simply have the spinner call out the actual number of the person to approach the plate.

SLAM DUNK SPELLING

Grades: 2–6

Purposes: To review and reinforce spelling words
To improve hand/eye coordination

Equipment: A foam rubber ball or wad of paper

Description: Divide the group into two equal teams. The first player from one team goes to the chalkboard. The leader gives him a word to spell, and if the child spells the word correctly a point is scored for his team. The second half of the game calls for the same player to shoot a foam rubber ball or paper wad into a trash can from a predeterminded distance. If the player makes the basket, he scores another point for his team. Thus, a player can score zero, one, or two points for his team on a given turn. The first player from the other team repeats the process and the game continues until each player has had a turn or a certain point total is reached.

Variations: (1) Have players from both teams play at the same time. In this version, after players have spelled their words a signal is given and both players pick up a ball and the first one to make a basket from the line scores the additional point for his team. (2) Play a "slam dunk" round where players use their fanciest dunk shot instead of shooting from the line.

COORDINATE CLUES

Grades: 2–6

Purposes: To introduce or reinforce coordinate graphing
To find "hidden" graph location
To enjoy an active math activity

Equipment: Index cards or paper of three different colors (as blue, yellow and white)
Masking tape
A marking pen

Description: Write large size numerals 0 through 9 on the blue cards. Repeat this process on the yellow cards. Tape these cards to two adjacent classroom walls so that they can be used to denote coordinate locations. For example, (0,0) will be in a corner and (5,5) should be near the center of the room, etc. Then write sequential clues on the white cards and hide all but the first one at their appropriate coordinate locations. Put them in interesting spots such as taped to the bottom of a chair or under a book. Place the first card at (0,0); it might read, "You are at (blue 0, yellow 0). Go to coordinate (blue 5, yellow 7) for your next clue. There is a surprise waiting, "IF you can find your way to the end of the coordinate trail." Allow the students to work in small groups as they seek each clue and then proceed to the next. At the end of the coordinate clue trail, each student might receive a simple surprise such as a paper badge labeled COORDINATE EXPERT, a coupon for an extra minute of recess, etc.

Variations: (1) Young students might be given just one clue that leads them to a single location. For example, if a yellow pencil had been hidden, they might be instructed to, "Find a long, thin, yellow object at (blue 3, yellow 7) and bring it to me." (2) Older students might be assigned the task of writing clues and setting up their own coordinate clue trails.

NOW IS THAT TRUE?

Grades: 2–6

Purposes: To provide exercise
To develop communication and listening skills

Equipment: None

Description: One child is chosen to stand in front of the room. All desks, including his, are occupied (remove or mark extra desks). The child in front begins to tell a story which may or may not be true. At some point near the end of the story, he says, "Now Is That True?" At this point all players change seats as the story teller attempts to find a vacant seat as well. The person left standing must guess whether the story was true or false correctly in order to become the new story teller. If he guesses wrong, the original story teller may tell another story. If the person standing guesses correctly, he becomes the new story teller. If the story teller does not get to a vacant seat, he must choose someone to come to the front and become the new story teller.

Variations: Eliminate the true or false rule, and have students tell creative stories, informational stories, or stories which relate to subjects being studied (in this version, have students say, "Change seats!").

VOCABULARY TWISTER

Grades: 2–6

Purposes: To enhance the study of reading vocabulary words and spelling
To provide an enjoyable physical activity

Equipment: One or more twister floor grids will be needed. The grids are best when constructed with reusable materials like an old bed sheet or a sheet of plastic, and written on with a permanent marking pen. However, temporary grids can be made with chalk and/or masking tape. Each letter of the alphabet is written on a grid space, and commonly used letters may be repeated at random. A six by six grid with spaces that are at least nine inches on a side is a very usable arrangement.

Description: Each three or four students are a vocabulary team. The teacher calls out a vocabulary word definition. The teams must then decide what the word is, how to spell it, and then show it on their grid by touching only the letters needed with their feet, hands, and/or nose. Repeated letters are indicated by having more than one student touch the needed letter(s). If the activity is to be scored, a point may be given for each correct team response, plus a possible bonus point to the team that is first.

Variations: (1) The letters of a word might be given in mixed order. The students must then unscramble it, and then touch the appropriate letters on the twister grid. (2) For longer words, five or six students may be on the grid together.

FINGER BASEBALL

Grades: 4–6

Purposes: To improve addition or multiplication skills
To promote cooperation

Equipment: Paper and pencil for each student
Scoring guide for each group (see below)

Description: Have students form groups of two. Each student then draws a baseball diamond on his paper. Each group needs to decide who will be "up" first. Next, the players make four simultaneous fist-to-palm movements and on the fourth movement each player displays a chosen number of fingers. (The game is similar in format to the "paper-scissors-rock" game.) The sum of both players' fingers indicates the outcome for the round. For example, if player A shows one finger, while player B shows four fingers, the outcome is five, which is a single according to the scoring guide. The process continues, with the batter keeping track of his men on base, and runs scored, until three outs are recorded. At this time, the opposing player is up to bat. The game can be terminated by setting a time limit, a total run limit, or by limiting the number of innings to be played.

SCORING GUIDE	
0	Single
1	Out
2	Double
3	Out
4	Triple
5	Single
6	Out
7	Home Run
8	Single
9	Out
10	Double

Variations: (1) Have students play with both hands, displaying zero to ten fingers rather than just zero to five (you will need to double the scoring guide to allow for 20 possible outcomes). (2) Have the students multiply fingers shown rather than adding them (extend the scoring to allow for 25 possible outcomes). (3) Have advanced students construct a scoring guide which allows 100 possible outcomes and play with both hands using multiplication.

DICTIONARY HIDE IT

Grades: 4–6

Purposes: To improve reading and vocabulary skills
To provide for the reinforcement of skills from various subject areas
To improve quickness and coordination

Equipment: An eraser (or any passable object) and a dictionary for each row

Description: Place a dictionary and an eraser on the front desk of each row. One person, from each row, comes forward and stands in front of his row, facing the front of the room. As the leader reads words from the dictionary the players in each row quickly pass the eraser up and down from one person to the next. As soon as the leader stops reading, the person with the eraser quickly hides it. At the same time, the person standing in the front of the row whirls around to identify who has the eraser before he can hide it. If the player at the front of the row identifies the person with the eraser on the first guess, they change places and the game continues. If the front player guesses incorrectly, he remains at the front of the row for a maximum of three turns, and then chooses someone to replace him. Establish a minimum number of words to be read by each player before whirling around.

Variations: (1) Have players read materials from different subject areas (math fact sheets, spelling lists, etc.). (2) Have the entire group play a round together. In this version, players pass the eraser from row to row. (3) For younger students, have players recite the alphabet or count to a certain number while the object is being passed.

PECULIAR PUNCTUATION

Grades: 4–6

Purposes: To reinforce the knowledge of proper punctuation
To improve listening skills
To increase flexibility

Equipment: None

Description: Have the players scatter about the play area. The leader asks for volunteers to suggest movements for certain types of punctuation. For example, a jump in the air might indicate a period, quotation marks might be shown by touching both hands on the ground while keeping the legs straight, and a question mark might be indicated by doing "the twist." The leader writes the decided upon movements on the chalkboard next to the appropriate pieces of punctuation. The leader then reads aloud a portion of any story and players listen carefully and display the proper movements when punctuation occurs. Students will soon be enjoying themselves and getting exercise while practicing their language skills!

Variations: (1) To play "Preposterous Punctuation" assign noises rather than movements for each item of punctuation. (2) Change the movements before playing another round. (3) Have student volunteers read to the group.

WHO AM I/WHAT AM I?

Grades: 4–6

Purposes: To provide review and reinforcement of concepts or vocabulary in any subject area
To provide mild exercise

Equipment: Some pieces of scrap paper
Several paper clips or pieces of tape

Description: Write the names of important people being studied in Social Studies on small pieces of paper and place them on a desk face down. Have all players go to the table and select one card and something to fasten it with. On a signal, have players walk briskly about the room in a random pattern. The leader signals players to stop, at which time they pair up with the person nearest them. Without showing his partner, each player fastens his name card to the back of the other's shirt. All players begin asking questions of their partner in an attempt to figure out the name of the person fastened to their back. After a short questioning session, the leader gives the signal to walk briskly again until the signal to stop is given, at which time players select new partners for questioning. The process continues until all players have successfully guessed who they are representing. People that finish before others may help answer questions for those still participating.

Variations: (1) Make cards for science, history, human interest, etc., and play Who or What Am I.
(2) Change the method of locomotion between questioning sessions (have players hop, jog, jump, etc.).
(3) Have the student collect and write the names of important people.

SPELLING BASEBALL

Grades: 4–6

Purposes: To provide review and reinforcement of spelling words
To improve hand/eye coordination

Equipment: A foam rubber ball of any size

Description: Divide the group into two teams. Set up a baseball diamond by placing pieces of paper marked 1st, 2nd, 3rd, and home on the ground. One team scatters about the play area. The other team is up to bat, and they form a line along the wall nearest 1st base. The first player steps forward, and the leader calls out a spelling word. If the student spells the word correctly, he earns an "at bat." The player makes a bat by clenching his fist, and the leader or another student pitches the ball. The player advances to first base if the ball is not *fielded cleanly* by the other team. The team in the field records an out by fielding the ball cleanly, whether it be a grounder, fly, or ricochet off the wall or ceiling. Players advance one base at a time, and the score is kept to establish a winning team. After the batting team makes their third out, the teams switch places and the game continues.

Variations: (1) Use the game to reinforce concepts, review for tests, etc., in other subject areas. (2) Play the game using regular baseball rules and allow players to walk briskly around the base paths. In this version, the fielding team must throw the ball to the appropriate base in time to record an out.

BOOT CAMP

Grades: 4–6

Purposes: To provide review and reinforcement for all concepts and subject areas
To improve overall physical fitness

Equipment: None

Description: Have each student write down a strenuous physical task (jump rope for 60 seconds, hop around the room 5 times without stopping, 25 push-ups, etc.). Put all the task challenges into a hat, bag, or box and mix them up. Divide the group into two teams. The leader asks each player a question about science, history, math, or any appropriate subject or concept. If the player answers the question correctly, he scores a point for his team. If someone fails to answer a question correctly, she must draw a piece of paper from the hat and perform the task successfully in order to score a point for his team. Thus, each player has two chances to score a point for his team. The team with the most points at the end of the play period wins, and may be given extra credit points in the grade book for the appropriate subject area.

Variations: (1) Allow students to perform a task, in addition to correctly answering a question, to earn bonus points for their team. (2) Play the game in smaller groups and allow group consultation before answers are given. In this version, the entire group must perform the task when incorrect answers are given.

GET THE MESSAGE

Grades: 4–6

Purposes: To correlate reading skills, direction finding, and physical activities
To increase motivation for reading and exercise

Equipment: Index cards with messages written on them
Large cards indicating North, South, East, and West

Description: Fasten the large North, South, East, and West cards to their respective classroom walls, and place the message cards (see examples below) in predetermined locations. Organize the students in small groups and rotate the student in charge at each turn. The groups may begin with any message card, carefully read what it says, complete the designated task, and then move to each of the other cards in turn. The teacher or leader should monitor the tasks as they are done to be certain that each message has been interpreted correctly.

> This is the northwest corner of the room. You're getting quite good at locating messages!
> Now, everyone touch your toes seven times.
> Super! Next, go to the card in the southeast corner of our room.

> Great, you have located the southeast corner!
> This time each person is to crabwalk to the teacher's desk.
> When you get there, look under the wastebasket for another message.

Variations: (1) To increase the difficulty level, the directions may be stated in terms of northeast and southwest, or even west northwest, etc. (2) The messages on the cards might be given as a code(s) that the students must decipher before they can do the task.

CODE BREAKER

Grades: 4–6

Purposes: To enhance reading and reasoning skills
To provide exercise

Equipment: Ten or more index cards with coded messages written on them (Code clues are to be given on the backs of the cards.)

Description: Organize the students in groups of two to four. Each group is to receive a card (see the following sample) with a coded message on it. They are to decode the message and do the physical activity indicated. If there is enough time, they may trade coded messages with another group.

```
Card #5
Do this:

  20,42,26,32,  2,38  16,18,14,16
2,38  50,30,42  6,2,28  38,18,48
40,18,26,10,38.
```

```
Code Clues:
A = 2,  B = 4 and F = 12
(back of card)
```

Variations: Advanced students may devise and share their own coded messages.

VI
Outrageous
Relays

JUMP ROPE RELAY

Grades: K–6

Purposes: To provide exercise for overall physical fitness
To improve coordination and agility

Equipment: A jump rope for each team

Directions: Each row is a team, and the teams line up at the back of the room. Have each team member jump rope to the front of his row and back.

Variations: (1) Have players turn around and jump rope backwards. (2) Have players stop at one end of the room and jump in place for a predetermined number of jumps.

BOUNCE-A-GOAL RELAY

Grades: K–6

Purposes: To improve coordination
To provide exercise

Equipment: Several balls of any type

Directions: Have players form four teams. A trash can is placed an adequate distance away, in front of each team. The object is to bounce a ball off the floor into the goal and get it back to the next player as quickly as possible. One point is scored for each successful shot. Total points are tabulated to determine the winning team.

Variations: (1) Have players throw the ball directly into the can instead of bouncing it. (2) Have players perform a task on the way back (dribble the ball, pass the ball between the legs at each step, etc.).

HOLIDAY RELAY

Grades: K–6

Purposes: To develop creative and artistic abilities
To increase multicultural awareness
To promote group cooperation

Equipment: None

Directions: Each row is a team. One at a time, each player runs to the board and draws a portion of a picture having to do with a given holiday (Christmas tree, Thanksgiving turkey, Easter bunny, etc.). The winning team is the one whose number one player has the chalk in his hand after all the team members have played. Minimum requirements for each drawing should, of course, be designated.

Variations: (1) Include holidays from foreign lands in order to stress multicultural awareness. (2) Rather than compete for the fastest drawing, play a round where time is not a factor. In this version have a judge, or have the whole class vote on the best team picture.

HAT PASS RELAY

Grades: K–6

Purposes: To improve small motor coordination and dexterity
To have fun

Equipment: Several rulers
Hats of any kind

Directions: Each set of two rows is a team. Each player has a ruler in his right hand. The first player in each team has a hat or cap on his ruler. On a signal, players receive and pass the hat, using only their rulers, to the end of the line. When the last player in the row receives the hat, he walks down the clear aisle to the front of his line, and the relay is continued until the team is back in its original position

Variations: Use objects that require more skill and concentration to pass (open milk cartons, a piece of yarn, etc.).

WILD ROLL RELAY

Grades: K–6

Purposes: To improve coordination and agility
To provide exercise

Equipment: Several balls of any type
One yardstick, bat, broom, or branch for each team

Directions: Each row is a team. A broom, bat, yardstick, or any stick is used to bat or push a ball to one end of the room. Players then pick up the ball and run back, with the ball in one hand and dragging the stick on the floor with the other hand.

Variations: (1) Have players shuffle backwards while batting the ball to their teams. (2) Have players hop while batting the ball down or back.

HIT THE SPOT RELAY

Grades: K–6

Purposes: To improve coordination
To provide exercise

Equipment: Several objects of any type to be thrown into the circle

Directions: Each row is a team. A circle is drawn an adequate distance from the front of each row. The first player takes three bean bags (or wads of paper, balled-up socks, etc.) and tries to throw them so that they land in the circle. Each player then runs and picks up the objects and returns them to the next player. One point is scored for each object that lands entirely in the circle. Total points are tabulated to determine the winning team.

Variations: (1) Vary the number, size, and shape of the objects to be thrown. (2) Have players use trick shots, or their non-dominant hand to throw.

CLEAN SWEEP

Grades: K–6

Purposes: To improve coordination and fitness
To have an enjoyable experience

Equipment: Several pieces of scrap paper
One broom for each team

Description: Two rows combine to form a team. Teams divide themselves into two groups, which line up at opposite ends of the room, facing each other. One broom and three to five pieces of crushed paper are needed for each group. On a signal, the first player sweeps all of the pieces of paper to the other end of the room, then hands the broom to his teammate, who sweeps the papers back to the other end of the room, and so on. First team to finish is the winner. Crush paper loosely so that it cannot be batted across the floor.

Variations: (1) If no brooms are available, play the game by having players use rulers, feet, or hands to sweep the papers. (2) End the game by having the losing team sweep all the paper to the trash can and throw it away.

TIRE PASS RELAY

Grades: K–6

Purposes: To increase flexibility
To promote group cooperation

Equipment: Several discarded bicycle tires

Description: Two or more circles are formed with an equal number of players in each. All players clasp hands, with two of the players in each circle clasping hands inside the tire. At a signal, the tire is passed around the circle without players letting go of their hands. The team that gets its tire back to the starting point first is the winner. Each player must squeeze through the tire as quickly as possible to move the tire around the circle.

Variations: (1) Have players form a large circle and start two tires on opposite sides. In this version, the object is for one tire to catch up with the other. (2) Have the students play the game with their eyes closed.

JUNK RELAY

Grades: K–6

Purposes: To promote teamwork
To have a great time

Equipment: Various classroom objects
Hoops, tires, newspapers, etc.

Description: Each row is a team. Teams line up at one end of the room. A hoop, mat, tire, or piece of newspaper is placed directly in front of each team (or a circle can be drawn with chalk) and another is placed at the other end of the room. Three to ten objects are placed in the hoops located directly in front of the teams (book, pencil, eraser, crayon, etc.). The first runner for each team must go to the near hoop, pick up all of the objects, take them to the far hoop and place them all inside of the hoop, and run back to tag the next runner. The next runner runs to the far hoop, picks up the objects, brings them back to the near hoop, and the procedure is repeated until all have had a turn. First team to finish wins.

Variations: (1) Have players go down and back in teams of two. (2) Play the game on 'desk clean out day' and have the players throw away objects they no longer need.

BAT THAT BALLOON

Grades: K–6

Purposes: To improve coordination
To provide exercise for overall physical fitness

Equipment: One balloon for each team

Description: Each row is a team. Each team is given one balloon. Each team member must travel down and back while keeping the balloon aloft by batting it repeatedly, being careful never to hold the balloon. The first team to successfully complete the task wins.

Variations: (1) Have players use only one hand. (2) Have players form pairs and go down and back with a partner. (3) Play a round where participants must use their feet instead of their hands to keep the balloon aloft.

READ AND RUN RELAY

Grades: K–6

Purposes: To improve reading skills
To provide exercise for overall physical fitness
To improve concentration

Equipment: Each team needs a copy of the same textbook

Description: Each row is a team. Select a paragraph or page from any textbook, and have players put the reading selection on the front desk of each row. On the signal to begin, the first person in each row stands up, reads the page or paragraph aloud as quickly as possible, then runs around his row four times and returns to his seat. Each player repeats the process, and the first team to finish wins.

Variations: (1) For younger students, have players count to ten, recite their ABC's, etc., before running around the row. (2) Change the task performed by participants after reading (dribble a ball around the row, hop around the row twice, etc.) (3) Change the material to be read (photocopied story, different textbooks, etc.).

TIRE TROT

Grades: K–6

Purposes: To provide exercise for overall physical fitness
To have fun

Equipment: One old bicycle tire or hoop for each team

Description: Each row is a team. A tire or hoop is placed at the far end of the room from each team. Players walk or jog to the hoop, jump inside of it, slide the tire up and over their heads, put the tire back on the ground, return to their team. Each player must repeat the process, and the first team to finish wins.

Variations: (1) Require players to do two or three "Hula Hoop" motions during their pass through the tire. (2) Have players do the reverse of the original motion. In this version, they pick up the tire, slide it over their heads and down to the floor, then return to their teams.

COIN CARRY

Grades: K–6

Purposes: To improve balance and agility
To provide exercise for overall physical fitness

Equipment: A penny or similar object for each team

Description: Each row is a team. Players must balance a penny on their forehead while walking as quickly as possible to the end of the room and back. If the object is dropped the player must stop, replace it, then continue on his way. The first team to finish successfully wins.

COINS

Variations: (1) Have players balance the coin in different spots (elbow, shoulder, foot, etc.). (2) Have players go in pairs with one as a guide and the one balancing the coin with eyes closed.

CRAZY CRINKLE

Grades: K–6

Purposes: To increase hand and forearm strength
To have fun

Equipment: A stack of old newspapers

Description: Each row is a team. Place an equal number of newspaper sheets at the front of each row. On the signal to begin, the first player from each team uses *one hand only* to crinkle up a sheet of newspaper until it forms a tight wad. When a player finishes, he moves to the end of the line and the next player continues the process. The first team to have all their sheets of newspaper wadded up wins.

Variations: (1) Play "Crazy Crinkle Basketball" in which players walk or jog down to a trash can and shoot their wadded up paper into the can for a basket, then come back and tag the next participant. (2) Play "Solo Crazy Crinkle" in which each player has his own stack of newspaper to crinkle; the first player to finish wins.

LINE BALL RELAY

Grades: 2–6

Purposes: To enhance physical fitness
To improve coordination

Equipment: A ball for each team

Directions: Each row is a team. One player from each team goes to the front of the room and faces his team. On a signal, the first person in each row stands up beside his desk and receives the toss by the person in the front of the room, and throws the ball back and sits down. As soon as he is seated, the next player goes as far as the front desk, receives and throws, sits down, and so on until the leader has thrown to all players in the row. He then holds up the ball. The row completing the throws first wins. Each player should get a chance to be the leader for a round.

Variations: Require throwers to use trick throws (one bounce, roll the ball between the legs, etc.). (2) Have catchers perform a task before throwing the ball back (bounce the ball five times, pass the ball between the legs in a figure eight pattern, etc.).

BLOW HARD RELAY

Grades: 2–6

Purposes: To promote teamwork and cooperation
To have fun

Equipment: Several feathers, ping pong balls, or other light objects

Directions: Two rows combine to form a team. At a signal, the first player in each team blows a feather (or ping pong ball) to the finish line, then picks up the feather and carries it back to the next player. Each team member repeats the procedure. The first team to finish wins.

Variations: (1) Have players blow the objects in pairs or threesomes (2) Use straws to direct breath against the ball.

ROW BOWL

Grades: 2–6

Purposes: To practice lead-up skills for bowling
To improve coordination

Equipment: Several balls of any kind
One bowling pin, plastic bottle, or plastic jug for each row.

Description: Each row is a team. Place a pin (or plastic Coke bottle) at the front of each row. The last player in each row stands beside his desk and rolls the ball (volleyball, playground ball, softball, etc.) down the aisle in an attempt to knock over the pin. He then retrieves the ball, sets up the pin if necessary, and hands the ball to the front seated player and takes that player's seat. The new bowler hurries to the back of the room and rolls the ball toward the pin, and repeats the procedure. Play until everyone has had a turn, or establish a point or time limit and play until one team reaches the limit.

Variations: (1) If materials are available, set up three objects for each row. (2) Have players try a game of bowling with their eyes closed.

BOX TO BACK RELAY

Grades: 2–6

Purposes: To promote teamwork and cooperation
To improve coordination and balance

Equipment: One box of any size for each team

Description: Two rows combine to form a team. Teams line up at the back of the room. The first two players from each team balance a box by pressing it between the back of the front player and the stomach of the rear player. The two must move quickly to the front of the room and back without letting the box fall. If the box falls, they must start over. When they finish, the box is handed to the next pair of teammates, and the procedure is repeated until all have had a turn. The first team to finish wins.

Variations: (1) Have players go up and back with the box pressed between their foreheads. (2) Have the players press the box between hips, shoulders, elbows, etc.

HEADS UP RELAY

Grades: 2–6

Purposes: To promote cooperation and teamwork
To increase coordination

Equipment: Various objects found in the classroom

Description: Each row is a team. Teams line up at one end of the room. Team members pair off. Each pair must walk sideways, with a foam ball or wad of paper placed between their foreheads, to the other end of the room and back. They give the object to the next pair, and the procedure is repeated until all have gone. The first team to finish is the winner. The game can be continued by changing the position of the object to be carried (between the chests, toes, knees, etc.). If a pair drops the object, they must start over.

Variations: (1) Vary objects to be carried from large to small, round to square, etc. (2) Have players complete relay while turned back to back.

DIZZIE LIZZIE RELAY

Grades: 2–6

Purposes: To provide exercise
To have a great time

Equipment: One baseball bat, yardstick, or rolled-up piece of construction paper for each team

Description: Each row is a team. A baseball bat, rolled-up piece of construction paper, or yardstick is placed at the far end of the room for each team. Each player must run to the stick, pick it up, bend down and place his forehead on it and spin around it three to five times, and then run back to tag the next player in line. The first team to finish is the winner.

Variations: (1) Have players go in pairs, with one player acting as escort to the dizzy player. (2) Have players attempt to perform a task on the way back (dribble a ball, walk a straight line, etc.).

FIFTY CENTS, BEAN BAG, ORANGE RELAY

Grades: 2–6

Purposes: To improve coordination and balance
To promote teamwork and cooperation
To have fun

Equipment: Coins
Bean bags
Pieces of fruit
Or any three substitute objects

Description: Each row is a team, and players pair off. One partner must walk or run the race, while the other partner must help keep the objects in their proper places as follows: $.50 in one eye, bean bag on head, and orange between knees (similar objects may be substituted). The partner actually in the race cannot handle any of the objects. Players go up and back, then transfer objects to the next pair. The race should be run twice so everyone gets a turn.

Variation: Have players try to run the relay with their eyes closed.

CARROT DIP RELAY

Grades: 2–6

Purposes: To improve flexibility and coordination
To promote cooperation
To have an enjoyable time

Equipment: A few carrots, some string, and some jars

Description: Each row is a team. One carrot apparatus must be made for each team. Drill a hole through the side of a carrot. Tie one end of a three foot string to the carrot and tie the other end to a belt. The first player puts the belt on and runs to a can or jar at the other end of the room, and then tries to place the carrot in the can by squatting down. The carrot should be hanging in back of the player. Once the carrot goes in the can, the player runs back to the next person in line and gives him the belt with carrot and the game continues until all have had a turn

Variations: (1) Players can go in pairs, and have one guide the carrot into the can. (2) Line up several cans and have the players dip their carrot in each one.

TEN TRIPS

Grades: 2–6

Purposes: To improve coordination
To encourage cooperation

Equipment: One ball (or other object for throwing) for each team

Description: To play this game, players may either remain in their seats, or circles of eight to ten players may be formed. One player from each team is chosen to be the thrower. On a signal, leaders throw a ball (or wad of paper) to each team member in turn. When the ball is returned by the last one, the leader calls, "One," indicating that the ball has made one complete round. The group finishing ten trips first wins.

Variations: (1) Introduce another ball into the pattern, in which case the thrower must work quickly to catch and throw one ball before the next one arrives. (2) Play a round where catchers can only use one hand to catch tosses.

FILL IT UP

Grades: 2–6

Purposes: To improve coordination and balance
To have fun

Equipment: One spoon and two containers for each team

Description: Each row is a team. Each team needs a container, filled with an equal amount of water, to place on a desk or chair at the front of their line. Have teams set an additional empty container on a desk or chair at the far side of the room. The object is for each team, using only a spoon to transport the water, to fill up the empty container at the far end of the room. The team that fills their container first wins.

Variations: (1) Use a different object to transport the water (eyedropper, half of a ping-pong ball), or use something other than water (paper clips, beans). (2) Have teams play a double round by requiring them to carry the water back to the original container. In this version, the team with the most water in the container at the end of the game wins.

VII
CHALLENGE
ACTIVITIES

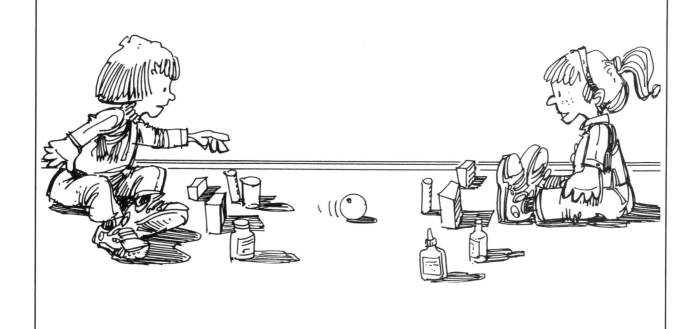

GIVE ME A LIFT

Grades: K–6

Purposes: To promote cooperation
To improve balance and strength.

Equipment: None

Description: Players sit in pairs on the floor facing each other. With feet flat on the floor and toes touching, they are to reach forward and grab hands. Then by pulling together they try to come to a standing position. They may also attempt to sit back down by using the procedure in reverse.

Variations: (1) Try the same procedure in groups of three or more. (2) Have advanced players attempt to spring out of the sitting position and spin a half turn in the air (so that they exchange positions) without letting go of their partner's hands.

BACK ME UP

Grades: K–6

Purposes: To promote cooperation
To improve balance and strength

Equipment: None

Description: The players need to be arranged in groups of two. They must then sit back to back on the floor and bring their knees up close to their chests. Next, they are to push their backs against each other as they attempt to stand up. They may also try to sit back down in the same fashion.

Variations: (1) Attempt the same procedure in groups of three, four, or more. (2) After a pair masters the original movement, they can attempt to move around the room in a halfway position. (3) Younger students can lock arms to make the procedure easier.

BACK-TO-BACK PUSH

Grades: K–6

Purposes: To improve strength and balance

Equipment: None

Description: Partners sit on the floor, back to back. By pushing with feet and hands, opponents try to force each other out of a circle drawn on the floor.

Variation: Play the game in pairs, in which case the one team has to force both opposing players out of the circle to win.

PRONE FEET-TO-FEET PUSH

Grades: K–6

Purposes: To increase upper body strength and endurance

Equipment: None

Description: Each person lies on his stomach, flat on the floor with his feet touching those of his opponent. By pushing with hands, each tries to push his opponent a certain distance.

BALL BETWEEN THE KNEES BLAST

Grades: K–6

Purposes: To improve strength and agility

Equipment: Two balls (or some type of soft objects) for each pair of players

Description: Both players squeeze a ball between their legs. They walk around the designated area and see which can knock the opponent's ball from between the legs first.

PRISONER

Grades: 4–6

Purposes: To improve strength
To promote teamwork and cooperation

Equipment: None

Description: Players form groups of five to ten. They form circles with hands clasped. One player goes into the center of the circle and attempts to break through. The person letting go replaces center person.

ARM-LOCK WRESTLE

Grades: K–6

Purposes: To increase strength and balance

Equipment: None

Description: Sitting back to back, opponents lean to their left in an attempt to make their partner's right arm or hand touch the floor.

KNOCK OUT

Grades: K–6

Purposes: To improve hand/eye coordination
To have fun

Equipment: Miscellaneous classroom objects (erasers, pencils, crayon boxes, etc.) and a small ball (tennis ball, handball, golfball, etc.) for each pair of players.

Description: Each player finds a partner. Partners squat or sit, facing each other, approximately 20 feet apart. Each player sets up an equal number of objects to be knocked over. The player with the ball gives it a roll toward the other player's objects in an attempt to knock one or more of them over. Objects that have been knocked over are cleared out of the way. The first one to knock over all the opponent's objects is the winner.

Variations: (1) Assign a point value for each object depending on its size and shape, and play to a certain point total. (2) Play the game between a row of desks instead of a clear space to increase the challenge.

HAND PUSH

Grades: K–6

Purposes: To improve balance and agility

Equipment: None

Description: Partners stand with toes touching and palms together at shoulder height. In this position, each tries to push the other's hands (or fake by changing force of push, backing hands off, etc.) until one player is forced to move one or both feet.

KING OR QUEEN OF THE MAT

Grades: K–6

Purposes: To improve strength, agility, and endurance
To have fun

Equipment: If the room is not carpeted, a large mat or rug is needed

Description: All players form a tight clump on a carpet or mat. Players assume the "crab-walk" position (sit down and then raise up on hands and feet). On the signal, all players attempt to push others off of the mat by pushing with their back. The last player on the mat is the winner.

Variation: Play the game in smaller groups and end with a match between the winners from each group.

MAKE A STAND

Grades: K–6

Purposes: To increase strength
To improve balance

Equipment: None

Description: Each player finds a partner and the two sit down back to back, knees bent, and arms linked. The object is for the pair to push against each other in an effort to stand up.

Variations: (1) Have players form groups of three, four, or any number and attempt the same feat as a large group. (2) Play the game in groups of three, in which two players attempt to stand up while the third player tries to foil the attempt.

SOCK BOP

Grades: K–6

Purposes: To provide exercise
To improve flexibility
To have a great time

Equipment: String and an old sock, (or similar object) for each player

Description: Pairs of players are designated to be opponents. Each ties a string around his or her waist with a balled-up sock tied to the end of the string. The opponents attempt to bop each other by moving their hips in order to swing their sock.

FUN JUG

Grades: 2–6

Purposes: To improve hand/eye coordination
To provide practice of lead-up skills for baseball

Equipment: A plastic milk jug and a bean bag, tennis ball, or wad of paper for each player

Description: The students or leader can cut the bottom off of the milk jugs. When the jugs are ready, each student will need a jug and an object to throw. Have players pair off and stand a few feet apart. The object of the game is for players to catch and toss the object back and forth successfully. Participants may move farther apart as they increase their accuracy.

Variations: (1) Have the players try trick throws and catches (behind the back, between the legs, etc.). (2) Have students form a circle and throw and catch across the circle in a random pattern.

BLOW BALL

Grades: 2–6

Purposes: To increase lung capacity
　　　　　　　To have fun

Equipment: A ping pong ball or wad of tissue or paper for each group

Description: Players form teams of two and stand on opposite sides of a desk. Books can be lined up on both edges of the desk for walls to keep the ball in play. The ball is placed in the middle of the desk and opponents attempt to blow the ping pong ball off the end of the other team's side of the table. Teammates spell each other periodically to avoid a shortage of air or dizziness. A point is scored each time a team blows the ball off the end of the opponents' side of the table.

Variations: (1) Have players place obstacles (erasers, crayons, etc.) on the desk to increase the challenge of the game. (2) Have both players on each team blow at the same time, or make teams of three or four.

AIR BIKE

Grades: 2–6

Purposes: To improve strength
To increase endurance

Equipment: None

Description: Each player finds a partner to challenge. Players support themselves by placing their hands on two desks or chairs, while lifting their feet off the ground. The object is for one player to outlast the other while pretending to peddle a bicycle in a suspended position. The game may also be played in small groups or with the entire class competing at the same time.

BALLOON BOXING

Grades: K–6

Purposes: To increase strength and stamina
                      To have fun

Equipment: String and a balloon for each player

Description: A balloon is tied around the waist of each boxer. Without clinching, players attempt to burst their opponent's balloon.

Variation: To end the game, allow the players to grasp their opponent's balloon in one hand and, when signaled, attempt to pop it by squeezing and/or twisting.

SIDE-BY-SIDE PUSH

Grades: 4–6

Purpose: To increase strength

Equipment: None

Description: Two persons lie side by side in a prone position. Each tries to push the other across a line drawn on the floor using only the side of his body.

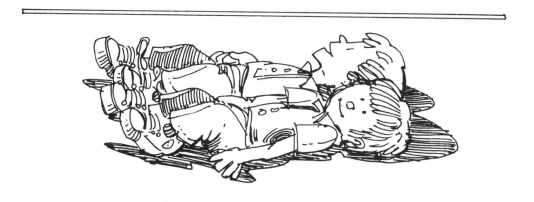

BACK TO BACK—RIGHT HAND BETWEEN LEGS

Grades: 4–6

Purposes: To improve balance, agility, and strength

Equipment: None

Description: Players stand back to back and place right hand between legs to grasp the hand of their partner who has assumed the same position. Players attempt to pull each other a certain distance.

LOCK-LEG WRESTLE

Grades: K–6

Purposes: To increase endurance and strength

Equipment: None

Description: Players should be of approximately the same size and they should complete stretching exercises before beginning. Then they lie flat on their backs and each raise one leg; they hook their legs together. The players attempt to turn each other over using only their hooked legs.

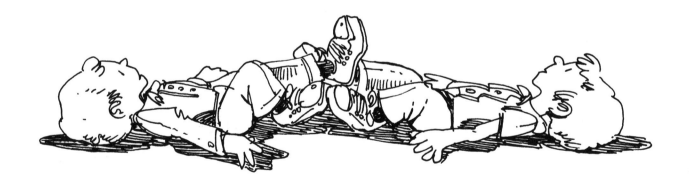

STORK WRESTLE

Grades: K–6

Purposes: To improve strength, balance, and agility

Equipment: Play in an open area away from furniture
A mat or rug surface can be utilized

Description: The players form a tight circle around the playing area. Two volunteers are selected by the teacher. These opponents each stand on one leg, with the other raised, and try to push or pull each other off balance. The game continues until one player must put both feet on the ground, or a designated time limit elapses. Two new players are designated and the game continues. Circle players are to catch anyone who begins to fall.

PILLOW POW

Grades: 4–6

Purposes: To enhance endurance and strength
To have fun

Equipment: Two old pillows or pieces of foam rubber

Description: Clear an area approximately ten feet by ten feet. Have players form a circle around this play zone. Two volunteer participants are then selected by the teacher to pick up the pillows and bop each other as many times as possible in a brief predetermined time period (1 minute or less). Play continues again as soon as two new participants are determined. Players in the circle call out words of encouragement to their favorite participants. The game continues until all volunteers have had a turn.

Variation: Certain body parts may be assigned as "point shots." In this version, players on the circle are the judges of legitimate scoring shots.

APPENDIX

Acquiring or Making Simple Equipment

Many of the activities in this book require no equipment at all. However, for those that do, the simple materials listed below may be easily collected or made. All are free or very inexpensive. In addition, some suggested substitutes are noted (in parentheses), or you may choose others that are similar. After acquiring these materials, you will be able to implement all of the activities from this book.

Beans	(paper clips, pennies, etc.)
Balloons	
Newspapers	
Balls	(rubber, tennis, basket, Nerf, or see the directions below for Making Foam Balls)
Bowling Pin	(cones, rolled-up magazines, etc.)
Plastic Soda Bottles	(2-liter Coke bottles)
Horseshoes	(foam rubber or Nerf)
Sheets, Blankets and Pillowcases	
String, Rope	
Beanbags	(wads of paper)
Boxes	
Old Brooms	(rolled-up magazines)
Sponges	(pieces of foam scrap)
Poker Chips	
Strips of Material	(paper strips)
Tin Cans	(plastic containers)
Clothespins	
Spoons	(ruler with cupped paper on end)
Carrots	
Paper Plates	
Plastic Milk Jugs	
Flashlight	
Straws	
Cotton Balls	(wads of paper)

Dice

Toilet Plungers

Hose Washers   (ring cut from an old bike tube)

Paper Clips

Hats

Feathers

Ping Pong Balls

Old Bike Tires and Hoops

Some of the most exciting activities call for *foam rubber* or *very soft* balls. Since many schools do not provide such balls, we have included directions for making them with donated materials. To make these very versatile balls, you will need to obtain old nylons and some soft stuffing material. Pillow stuffing works best, but wadded paper or other soft material can be substituted. Then put them together in the following manner:

1. Cut off the legs from nylons leaving the maximum length.

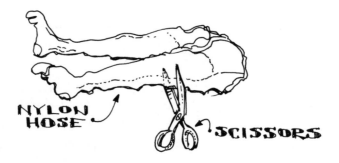

2. Insert a softball-size wad of stuffing into the foot section of a nylon.

3. Twist the nylon several times to enclose the wad of stuffing.

4. Push the wad back through the leg of the nylon.

5. Twist the ball section several times and send it back through the leg of the nylon again.

6. Repeat the process until most of the nylon is used. Then tie a knot in the end of the nylon and trim off any excess.

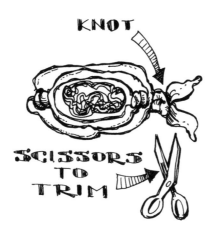

If your students are able, you may want them to help make the balls. The ball making project might also be a lead-up art/craft activity, with the balls being used in a game as soon as they are completed. You can be certain that a class set of these "foam" balls will provide considerable exercise and enjoyment throughout the year.

The authors are acutely aware of the efforts by teachers to collect all sorts of classroom materials in order to enhance their students' education. Most times parents are also willing to help with the collection of needed items. Thus, a sample request letter, that you may want to make use of, is provided (see the following page). The collection of these basic materials will be a most worthwhile investment for you and your students. They will provide for a great deal of enjoyment and exercise during the school year.

Equipment Request Letter

Dear Parents,

Our class is collecting a set of homemade physical education equipment. We can use materials that may be in your home, but which are no longer being used. Our goal is to have enough equipment so that all of the students will be able to actively participate in each activity. You can help us to accomplish our goal by donating any of the following items:

1. _____
2. _____
3. _____
4. _____
5. _____

We appreciate your help. These materials will provide a great deal of exercise and enjoyment during the school year.

Sincerely,

Selected References

Bryant, Rosalie and Eloise McLean Oliver, *Complete Elementary Physical Education Guide.* West Nyack, New York: Parker Publishing Co., Inc., 1974.

Bryant, Rosalie and Eloise McLean Oliver, *Fun and Fitness Through Elementary Physical Education.* West Nyack, New York: Parker Publishing Co., Inc. 1967.

Cotler, Harold L., *Galaxy of Games, Stunts, and Activities for Elementary Physical Education.* West Nyack, New York: Parker Publishing Co., Inc., 1980.

Kamiya, Art, *The Elementary Teacher Handbook of Indoor and Outdoor Games.* West Nyack, New York: Parker Publishing Co., Inc. 1985.

Overholt, James L., *Dr. Jim's Elementary Math Prescriptions: Activities/Aids/Games to Help Children Learn Elementary Mathematics.* Glenview, Illinois: Scott, Foresman and Co. (Goodyear Division), 1978.

Tillman, Kenneth G. and Patricia Rizzo Toner, *What Are We Doing in Gym Today?* West Nyack, New York: Parker Publishing Co., Inc., 1983.